FOR THE
SAKE OF
ARGUMENT

FOR THE SAKE OF ARGUMENT

HOW TO DO PHILOSOPHY

ROBERT M. MARTIN

broadview press

BROADVIEW PRESS www.broadviewpress.com
Peterborough, Ontario, Canada

Founded in 1985, Broadview Press remains a wholly independent publishing house. Broadview's focus is on academic publishing; our titles are accessible to university and college students as well as scholars and general readers. With over 600 titles in print, Broadview has become a leading international publisher in the humanities, with world-wide distribution. Broadview is committed to environmentally responsible publishing and fair business practices.

The interior of this book is printed on 100% recycled paper.

Library and Archives Canada Cataloguing in Publication

Martin, Robert M., author
    For the sake of argument : how to do philosophy
/ Robert M. Martin.

Includes bibliographical references.
ISBN 978-1-55481-337-7 (paperback)

    1. Philosophy—Introductions. 2. Philosophy—Study and teaching.
3. Methodology. 4. Rhetoric. 5. Reasoning. 6. Logic. I. Title.

BD21.M368 2016   168   C2016-906221-X

Broadview Press handles its own distribution in North America
PO Box 1243, Peterborough, Ontario K9J 7H5, Canada
555 Riverwalk Parkway, Tonawanda, NY 14150, USA
Tel: (705) 743-8990; Fax: (705) 743-8353
email: customerservice@broadviewpress.com

Distribution is handled by Eurospan Group in the UK, Europe, Central Asia, Middle East, Africa, India, Southeast Asia, Central America, South America, and the Caribbean. Distribution is handled by Footprint Books in Australia and New Zealand.

Broadview Press acknowledges the financial support of the Government of Canada through the Canada Book Fund for our publishing activities.   Canada

Edited by James Thomas
Cover and interior design by John van der Woude, JVDW Designs

PRINTED IN CANADA

CONTENTS

INTRODUCTION
PLEASE READ
THIS INFORMATION

This is a manual for philosophy students, and those who would like to be. It's designed as a practical handbook for philosophical thinking, writing, and talking. There are some philosophical discussions in here, used as examples, but this book won't teach you any philosophy. (Though I'll often give you references to philosophical reading sources for these examples, in case you want to look at them.)

This book is intended to teach you how to *do* philosophy. Doing philosophy means reading it, which you don't need to be told how to do, but (more importantly) talking and writing it, which you might need to learn about. Most of what's in here is about arguing—not regular arguing, but *philosophical* arguing, the most basic philosophical technique. You have to know how to do it if you're going to do philosophy, if you're going to have some well-developed philosophical beliefs.

You'll see pretty soon that this book isn't like most other philosophy books you've read. Those books are formal, a little bit distant, mostly straight-faced, and sometimes a bit pompous or pretentious. This one is very informal. It has a lot of asides, jokes, anecdotes, digressions, oddments, and entertainments in it. It's opinionated. It wanders around a bit. It talks to you something like the way a person you know would talk to you. This is not the way you're supposed to write philosophy books, but this book is not exactly one of them.

There are a lot of digressions and fooling around.

 Some of that takes place in text boxes like this. The reason this stuff is separated from the main text is so you can ignore it

*(if you're in a hurry, or don't enjoy that sort of thing) without
missing much of the main material.*

But if this material in text boxes is really unimportant, you might
wonder, why did the author of this book put all of this in?

A good question. I got some very good advice from the publisher of
the first philosophy book I wrote, and it's this: avoid footnotes (except
for bibliographical references) and text box asides; if what you want
to say has some importance, put it in the main text; if it's not important, then leave it out. So this, then, is your first ADVICE-NUGGET for
writing philosophy, in a small assignment, a larger essay, or a book:
STICK TO THE POINT. Leave out irrelevancies. Don't fool around.

That advice is completely ignored in this book. How come? Is
it because the author is self-indulgent and out of control? Yes, but
there's more to it than that. This is a book for current and future
philosophy students and people like them: that is, for people who
are intelligent and curious about all sorts of things. And who like
to read something provocative, or odd, or funny. And who like to
stay up too late with people like them chatting and discussing and
disagreeing about a huge and random set of topics, armed with that
most important philosophical tool: beer.

 *That comment about beer is not just a joke. It has important
historical significance. One of the most important works in
the history of philosophy is Plato's* Symposium, *the (fictitious)
record of a philosophical discussion at a get-together lasting
well into the night and featuring a great deal of wine. (The
ancient Greeks preferred wine to beer, but what did they know?)
In fact, 'symposium' originally meant* drinking party. *This sort
of event, including philosophical and other sorts of discussion,
often with the addition of entertainment and various kinds
of fooling around, was an important feature of ancient Greek
social life. I hope it's an important feature of yours too.*

So you might see the text box portion of this book as a sort of
late-night chat, but minus the beer, which its broad-viewed but nar-
row-minded publisher refused to provide free with each copy.

CHAPTER 1

TRUTH

I said this book is about argument. But why argue about philosophical beliefs? It's a free country; everyone's entitled to their own opinion, right?

Well, that depends.

First of all, we should distinguish between two sorts of opinion. One sort has nothing to do with truth. Examples:

- chocolate ice cream is much better than vanilla
- classical music sucks
- the Toronto Maple Leafs are the only hockey team to root for
- Three Stooges movies are hilarious
- Justin Bieber is just the cutest thing there is

I don't mean that these are false. I mean that they're neither true nor false. It's stupid to argue about any of these opinions (although, for sure, people disagree about them). You are, of course, entitled to these opinions, and you shouldn't really care if somebody feels differently. So stop getting mad at those Montréal Canadiens fans.

But other opinions are either true or false. These are opinions that are called *beliefs*. If you believe that the Franco-Prussian War began in 1875, then you're right or you're wrong. (You're wrong. It was 1870.) If someone has a different opinion, then at least one of you is wrong. If it makes any difference to either of you, then you'll want to make some efforts to find out what the year really was. All this is entirely out of place, of course, when it's a matter of ice cream preference.

WHY TRUTH?

But does it matter to you whether your belief about that date is true or not? *Should* it matter? What's so good about having true beliefs?

One reason is that, by and large, having a true belief about something is better for you—has better effects—than having a false belief, or no belief at all, about it. This is especially clear when it comes to everyday matters. If you believe your plane leaves at 4 p.m. and arrive at the airport in plenty of time for that, but in fact your plane was scheduled for 10 a.m., you're in trouble. And you'll also be in trouble if you have no beliefs at all about when your plane leaves (and don't try to find out).

Sometimes, however, having a true belief is more harmful. For example, imagine that the plane you missed crashed after take-off; your life was saved by your mistaken belief. But the consequences of true beliefs are *usually* better than those of false ones.

BULLSHIT

This is now an acceptable technical term in philosophy. I'm not kidding. It has been ever since the publication, in 2005, of *On Bullshit*,[1] by the distinguished Princeton philosopher Harry Frankfurt. The book is not a joke either. It's a serious treatment of what Frankfurt takes to be a growing and dangerous trend: talking and writing with no concern about truth. Bullshitters, then, are different from liars. Liars recognize the difference between truth and falsity, and try to get others to believe what's false. Bullshitters don't care what's true or not, and pay no attention to truth or falsity in what they say. They just make up things, and say them to suit their purposes.

Frankfurt thinks that bullshitting is on the increase. He thinks that part of the blame for this is the increasing number of situations in which people who know nothing at all about a subject are encouraged to give their opinions about it. Several situations like this come to mind. School children, in order not to injure their delicate self-esteem, are nowadays encouraged to express any unfounded opinion they like; they're praised by the teacher, and their opinions go uncorrected. The Internet provides endless venues for ignorant opinionation. There are loads of "call-in" programs on the radio, where people's baseless but nevertheless strong views can be broadcast to a large audience.[2] Frankfurt points at postmodern antirealism, a family of views recently infecting the academic humanities, the central idea of which is that there is no such thing as the facts: there's only what appears to you, coherent with—in fact, generated by—your particular ideological/social/economic/gender position. (I doubt, however, that this movement has had much effect outside the Groves of Academe.)

> *Several political commentators have remarked on the growing prevalence of bullshit in political campaigning, frequently mentioning Donald Trump's tendency to say, for effect, whatever he wants, with no concern about whether what he says is true.[3] Compare this with a slightly different phenomenon in political talk: truthiness. This word, coined by American T V satirist Stephen Colbert, refers to an assertion a person makes because it feels right, not because it's backed by evidence or logic—the truth he wants to exist. Colbert attributed this characteristic to assertions made by George W. Bush. And, of course, both of these are different from Nixon's flat-out lying.*

Frankfurt is upset about the increase in bullshit. He thinks that getting used to saying and hearing bullshit undermines our capacity to care about the truth of what we believe—so it's more dangerous than lying.

Frankfurt is right to be upset about political bullshit. There are consequences, often very important ones, of what politicians say.

But wait a minute. Let's be careful here. There are two possibilities for interpreting what the Donald says. One is that he'll just say anything, whether he believes it or not, as long as it has the effect he wants. This is something like lying but not exactly. Another is that he actually believes what he says, but he has failed utterly to take proper care—any care at all, apparently—to assure himself that his beliefs are really true. Both might be counted as bullshit. When we (finally!) get around to thinking about talk and writing in philosophy, we'll consider both kinds of philosophy bullshit.

BELIEFS OF NO CONSEQUENCE

All right. Let's concentrate on the second kind of bullshit: failure to take appropriate care to make sure that what you believe is true. The question we've been looking at—maybe you've forgotten, and no wonder—is why we should worry about whether our beliefs are really true. When there are good consequences for true beliefs, or bad consequences for false, then that's the answer. But there are lots of cases in which what you believe has no practical import—that belief about the Franco-Prussian War, for example. Or the belief that the planet Neptune has the third-largest diameter of any planet in the Solar System, or that the smallest prime number larger than 829 is 833. These beliefs are false (Jupiter, Saturn, and Uranus are larger in diameter; and the next prime number is 839—Are you glad I told you?), but it's hard to imagine how having these beliefs, or no beliefs at all about these matters, might do you any harm, or how you'd benefit from a true belief about the war, the planet, or the number. What good will it do you to have the (true) belief that in 1938 the state of Wyoming produced one-third of a pound of dry edible beans for every man, woman, and child in the nation?

 This bean factoid actually had considerable practical application. The single sentence reporting it was used as a filler (a tiny item inserted at the bottom of a newspaper column to take up empty space) in a scrappy little New York newspaper, the Village Voice, *that used it constantly during the 1960s, sometimes three or four times in a single issue.*

But it seems that even when there's no prospect of benefit resulting from a true belief, or harm resulting from a false one, some people want to have true beliefs anyway. Why? Well, they just value truth, period. True beliefs sometimes have, for some people, what philosophers call *intrinsic value*; that is, they are just good in themselves, not good for anything else. (The contrast here is with *instrumental value*.) (Scratching where it itches has purely intrinsic value.)

From a biological/evolutionary point of view, it makes sense that we see intrinsic value in having true beliefs. The whole biological point of our belief-forming mechanisms is to get beliefs right—any sorts of beliefs. Truth is where the survival advantage usually lies, and that explains why these mechanisms evolved.

 This is somewhat oversimplified. We can distinguish between mechanisms that are designed primarily to maximize the organism's true beliefs, and those designed primarily to minimize the organism's false beliefs. Which is more advantageous depends on circumstances (the value of a true belief, the harm of a false belief). Further, when it would take too much time or effort to do either, something less than maximizing/minimizing would be more advantageous.

They're general mechanisms that don't pick and choose among different contexts. So it's normal to have some curiosity—some desire to have true beliefs and avoid false ones—even in areas where there seems to be no advantage or disadvantage in believing anything or nothing.

The fact that evolution has built us (some of us) to care about the truth of our beliefs (some of them) does not justify that care. It may explain why we care, but it doesn't show why somebody who doesn't care should. This is a general problem with justification. When (it seems) we've reached ground floor—when something is sometimes desired just intrinsically—how can we prove to people who don't that they should find it desirable? Maybe we can't. Suppose you had a friend who thought that the Franco-Prussian War began in 1860 because she just sort of remembers having learned that in high school a decade ago, and you wanted to convince that person to take more care to make sure that that belief was true. Historians are interested in getting these things right, but why should your friend be? If your friend (like many others) isn't really worried about the possibility she's gotten the date wrong, then maybe that's the end of the story.

OKAY BUT REMEMBER WE'RE TALKING ABOUT PHILOSOPHY

Right.

So now there are three possible categories for philosophical opinions:

1. There isn't any question of truth or falsity here at all.
2. Truth and falsity do apply, and there are consequences which make it better to have true opinions. Philosophical truths can have instrumental value.
3. Truth and falsity do apply, but having true opinions just has intrinsic value for some people.

It's a popular view that philosophical opinions fall into category (1). This categorization is expressed by the saying, "Everybody's got their own philosophy." The implication here is that there's no arguing about philosophical opinions, because they're something like individual matters of taste. Compare "Everybody's got their own taste in ice cream."

But what is this "philosophy" that everyone's supposed to have? Sometimes people mean by a "philosophy" a guiding principle for your life, or a short and pithy description of your general outlook.

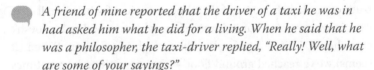

A friend of mine reported that the driver of a taxi he was in had asked him what he did for a living. When he said that he was a philosopher, the taxi-driver replied, "Really! Well, what are some of your sayings?"

It's possible (but unlikely) that you have one of those philosophies (or should). Most people don't have one of them. They never think about an overriding general principle for their lives, and just live them one day after another. Is there something wrong with this? Socrates (who you're supposed to think is the greatest philosopher ever) allegedly said: "The unexamined life is not worth living." Is that supposed to mean that you're better off dead if you run your life without thought to your overriding general principles? Well, that's crazy. That sort of self-examination stands a good chance of rendering you incapable of doing anything, paralysed with self-consciousness, or at least of making you the kind of person others want to avoid.

Anyway, if you care to have one of these, you can make one up any way you like. Go right ahead. Most of the books in the

*"philosophy" section of your local bookstore are designed to
help with this. But here's an unexpected source of help with
finding your "philosophy": a cosmetics company, which owns
the Philosophy.com domain, offers six different perfumes in
their My Philosophy series, each having a name which is a
full sentence expressing a different philosophy. One flavour of
perfume is called* I see the world with love and compassion
(the corresponding smell is "creamy vanilla"). Another is I
always give kindness without expectation *("sparkling musk").
It's unclear whether you're expected to choose the smell that
corresponds to the philosophy you already have, or if smelling
that way is supposed to cause you to adopt that philosophy.
See their web page "What My Philosophy Perfume Is Right
For You?"*

Disappointingly for some students, however, very little of philosophy—as practised by academic philosophers—aims at providing that
sort of thing. What this book is about is not that kind of "philosophy."
What's called "philosophy" in this book is more serious, more complicated, and much more interesting. Everyone does *not* have one of
these. And you shouldn't just say or think anything you like. Truth
and falsity do matter here.

A second popular view of philosophy is that it aims not at truth
but rather at psychological benefit: the production of a "philosophical attitude"—one of acceptance or acquiescence or submission
or calm in the face of difficulty or disappointment or disaster. That
would all be nice, I suppose, but academic philosophy is no good at
providing any of that, and doesn't even try. The professional philosophers I know are no better than anyone else at taking a "philosophical attitude." Difficulties and disappointments leave me a wreck.

 *So where can you look for this? The novelist Kurt Vonnegut Jr.
gives his personal answer: "Comedians and jazz musicians
have been more comforting and enlightening to me than
preachers or politicians or philosophers or poets or painters or
novelists...." Add other kinds of music, and I think this would be
widely applicable.*[4]

A third popular view is that philosophy is bullshit: idle speculation with no care for truth. That's reflected when people say things like, "Well, we should stop philosophizing about this, and actually do some real investigation." Real philosophers have the same kind of disdain for that kind of philosophizing as the rest of the world does.

> But the idea that philosophers just indulge in other-worldly speculation detached from earthly realities has a long and distinguished history. During his lifetime, Socrates appeared as a character in Aristophanes' comedy The Clouds (419 BCE), suspended in a basket up in the air. One of his disciples reports, "a lizard caused him the loss of a sublime thought.... One night, when he was studying the course of the moon and its revolutions and was gazing open-mouthed at the heavens, a lizard crapped upon him from the top of the roof."[5]

Philosophy has a bad reputation, doesn't it?

CONSEQUENCES?

But philosophy actually has some areas which are of great use—where true philosophical belief makes you better off, and where philosophical progress may actually produce benefits. The instrumental value of philosophical truth stems largely from the way it is able to figure out the (sometimes unconscious) cognitive frameworks and presuppositions of other fields; in Bertrand Russell's words, the aim of philosophy is to produce "the kind of knowledge which gives unity and system to the body of the sciences, and the kind which results from a critical examination of the grounds of our convictions, prejudices, and beliefs."[6] It aims at finding out, for example:

- how biology does taxonomy
- how cosmology determines the origins of the universe
- what the criteria are of a good scientific explanation
- how aesthetics evaluates works of art
- the general principles of right and wrong
- what justice is

- when children or cognitively disabled persons might be considered responsible for making medical decisions for themselves
- the basic principles of logic and good reasoning (these were the theoretical basis for developing computer technology)
- how judges should understand the basis of written law
- whether animals have what it takes to be granted rights

If we can uncover the basic beliefs, methodologies, presuppositions, structure, values behind some area of study or activity, then we might be able to help that area to proceed more efficiently; or, on the other hand, to raise questions about how consistent, efficient, worthwhile the basis of that activity is.

However, like any pure science, philosophy has large areas in which true belief appears to have only intrinsic value. That's okay! And it's too bad that universities nowadays are concentrating so much on the most applied disciplines—those who claim the loudest that they're *useful* (and by that they mean moneymaking)—to the detriment of the pure sciences and humanities. Just as historians want to know the (useless) facts about the Franco-Prussian War, philosophers want to know the philosophical facts. I admitted above that there's no way of convincing somebody who isn't interested that philosophical facts without instrumental value are worth knowing; but fortunately in philosophy, as in every other discipline, there are people who just happen to be interested in knowing those facts. May I assume that you, having read this far, are one of those people? If so, then, we'll now get down to the main business of this book which is to talk about the tool for seeking philosophical truth: argument.

CHAPTER 2

THE RIGHT WAY TO ARGUE

AND THE WRONG WAY TO ARGUE

One sort of activity called "argument" is a nasty business. It's a heated, even angry, disagreement. It can include sarcasm, raised voices, or slamming doors. The classical pre-divorce kitchen argument involves broken dishes.

This sort of toxic argument—we'll call it argument☠—arises from a disagreement between two people, but it has nothing to do with finding out which of the two is right. It's not like a prizefight, designed to find out which of two boxers is better, because a prizefight can have a winner. These arguments☠ never have winners. In an argument☠ between Felix and Freda, suppose Felix gives up, or is bullied into submission. This constitutes no progress in establishing that Freda was right. Freda may feel victorious, but (in a moment of rationality, which probably won't arrive soon, and may never arrive) she will realize that this victory establishes nothing about the correctness of her side of the disagreement. And when Felix gives up, even if he tells Freda that he guesses she was right, inside he's no more—probably less—convinced of that than when they started arguing☠. Anyway, what most often happens is that nobody gives in, both people go away mad, and everyone is worse off.

The kind of argument we're interested in is quite different. If it gets angry, then something has gone wrong. Participants in this sort of argument need to be open-minded—not *empty*-minded, but interested in testing their own beliefs, learning what's behind contrary beliefs, and, possibly, changing their minds. They try to give good reasons to support their beliefs, and to show why opposing views are wrong. The object of the game here is truth, not winning. Dishes won't get broken.

When talking about argument from now on, I'll mean this sort (unless I include the ☠).

A SOCIAL ACTIVITY

There are various kinds of procedures that you can do, all by yourself or with the help of others, to make your own beliefs more likely to be true. If you think that the Franco-Prussian War began in 1865, but you want to make sure, you can look it up in a reliable encyclopedia, or ask a historian. If you want to satisfy yourself that your impression that you locked the car is really true, you can go test the handle or ask someone else to do it.

Arguing for a belief is a special sort of procedure you go through to make it more likely that the belief is true. At core, it's a social activity like a cocktail party or a rock concert. I mean that it's basically a matter of interaction between humans, not something you normally do alone. It happens when two people disagree about some belief, and there's an effort by at least one of them to try to change the other's mind. Or when one person believes something that the other person doesn't have any opinion about, and the first person tries to convince the second.

Can you do it all by yourself? There are cases in which you haven't decided whether something is true or false, or in which you're pulled in both ways. You consider the reasons for and against what you're undecided about. (It's stretching things to call this an argument with yourself.) But it's usually better to have someone else to discuss things with, and better still if the two of you have opposing beliefs you'd like to test. When someone else is involved, then you're much more likely to discover reasons for or against that you haven't thought of, and to see what's wrong (or right) about what you think.

Philosophers love to find other philosophers who disagree with them.

 Well, a lot of philosophers do. Some, of course, are lazy. Others are so strongly attached to their beliefs and ideologies that they prefer to surround themselves with like-minded philosophers,

and to avoid argument. They will also be the professors who will treat only their own positions seriously in lectures to their students, and who will give higher grades to student papers that agree with them. This turns philosophy into a pep rally for one position. Watch out for these philosophers, and avoid them.

You'll find some philosophers busy arguing with each other, even in their spare time, and writing argumentative papers at a great rate, hoping to read them at a seminar or conference, or to have them published in a journal.

Philosophy is, in fact, unusual in among the disciplines in the extent of its reliance on argument. It's the main way philosophers have of testing their beliefs. Chemists for example, by contrast, have their laboratories, where they can go test their beliefs by doing experiments. But interpersonal argument is the philosophers' laboratory.

The history of philosophy bears this out. Philosophers are all sure that, if their writing gets any notice, there will be strenuous arguments against their positions by others. Sometimes they even invite counter-argument to appear with their own writing.

René Descartes sent the manuscript of his Meditations *to several philosophers hoping they'd reply with objections and counter-arguments. They did, and their objections and his replies were published together in the book.*

A few philosophy journals seek counter-arguments from other philosophers to publish next to their articles, in the same issue. But usually counter-arguments by other people don't accompany publication, so good philosophers try to imagine these responses, and present them fairly and with whatever sympathy they can manage, before trying to explain what's wrong with them.

The articles in Aquinas's Summa Theologica *all begin with the a statement of the position he'll disagree with, followed by the best arguments Aquinas can think of against his own position; then he gives his position, and replies to each of the arguments against it. Plato, not for nothing called the Father of Philosophy, wrote in dialogue form, with different speakers advocating and defending different positions and a lot of back-and-forth argument.*

What we have been emphasizing, and what is borne out by examination of great philosophical writing, is that it is never merely expression of the author's opinion. It is always accompanied by the best justifications the author can conjure up, to defend these positions. And because argument is essentially a social phenomenon, philosophers talk to each other—argue against each other—even if they have to imagine the objections themselves. But this sort of solipsism usually doesn't last long. It's usually not difficult to find a philosopher who disagrees with you. And publication of your ideas will often result in counter-arguments from someone else.

So if you're in a community of philosophers, you can pretty well count on some pretty good opposition to what you say. This is good news. Philosophical argument against your position is not disrespect—quite the reverse. It's treating it as worthy of serious consideration and objection. Don't be upset when someone argues with you, and don't be shy about arguing with others.

Are all groups of philosopher "communities"? The phrase 'the [X] community' is often just a trendy meaningless substitute for '[X]s'. On a radio interview I heard a naturalist say, "the bird community eats the mosquito community." But when things are as they should be, there is a philosophical community: philosophers really do work together, perhaps more than in any other discipline. They find others they can talk to, often at other universities. But this doesn't mean that every bunch of philosophers is all peace, love, and good vibes. On the contrary: philosophy departments, like all academic departments, are often like badly dysfunctional families. The motto that sums up most academic departments is "a tempest for every teapot."

It's an odd—almost paradoxical—situation. On the one hand, you're trying to back up your position as strongly as you can—to anticipate and disarm any possible objections. On the other, you seek out philosophers who disagree with you, and can give you really good criticism and counter-argument.

Anyway, the takeaway lesson here is this. When thinking about what philosophical ideas you're going to believe, and when writing or talking about them, follow the lead of the great philosophers, and try to anticipate and present arguments counter to your position. Doing this will make for better philosophy.

RESPECT AND OPEN QUESTIONS

Sometimes an argument can become a heated and nasty argument. You can see how it's important that this not happen. But it's possible to avoid it. All that's necessary is that you show the proper respect for your arguing opponent, and for positions in opposition to yours. If you really understand the issues, you'll treat opposing views with respect. The reason for this is an unusual fact about philosophy: just about every philosophical question has a variety of different respectable attempts at answers—attempts that each have some clever arguments supporting them. This is true even for a position that looks flat-out stupid to you. Instead of just dismissing that position, you should ask yourself how some very smart people managed to believe it. Try to understand what sort of basic principles and presuppositions and methodology those philosophers were using, to find out where smart people went wrong.

Every question in philosophy is *open*. This doesn't mean that there's no progress, or that it's pointless to try to come up with an answer, or that every attempt to answer the question is just as good as any other. Even though the old questions in philosophy are still there after 2,000 years or more, philosophers, building on what's been said before, keep coming up with better, more ingenious, more satisfactory answers; and these lead to more ingenious counter-arguments.

This situation—open questions everywhere—is unusual. Consider what often happens in science, by contrast. An introductory science textbook contains just about nothing but widely accepted scientific fact. Scientists don't argue about the facts in this book, and you're expected to accept everything it says. Introductory chemistry students who take a critical attitude to the assertion that the atomic number of molybdenum is 42, and look for counter-arguments, are making a mistake. By contrast, every position discussed in introductory philosophy is controversial, with arguments supporting it, and attacking it—and all those arguments deserve your respect.

Another contrast between science and philosophy is what often happens at the cutting-edge of each discipline. Imagine a biologist who finds out the details of the life of a practically unknown spider living deep in the Amazon jungle. She gets that information published in *The Journal of Arachnology*.

 Yes, this is a real journal. Their website tells authors to deposit "specimens of species used in your research" in a recognized academic institution—an instruction rarely found in websites for philosophy journals.

Everybody accepts what this scientist says. Nobody puts up an argument. Anybody who writes something based on her discoveries cites her article as the expert source for the facts. Note that this sort of acceptance of people as experts, with citation of what they assert—routine procedure in science—never happens in philosophy.

The fact that just about everything in philosophy is controversial, from the beginning level up, does not imply that you must remain agnostic—neutral—about answers. When you encounter a position somebody is presenting, it's entirely acceptable—even desirable—for you to decide whether you think it's right or wrong, and, if possible, to bring in your own reasons for that reaction. Of course there's nothing wrong with remaining neutral in the face of compelling arguments pulling in opposite directions, especially in an area you don't feel you know well enough. But whenever you encounter somebody's position, and that person's supporting arguments, the appropriate attitude is to be asking yourself all along whether what that person says is correct.

But when you disagree with some position, or take a side in a debate, it's very important that you treat the other side(s) with respect. This is the case whether you're engaging in philosophical debate with someone else face-to-face, or dealing with opposing positions and their rationale in the argumentative writing you produce.

What's involved in treating an opponent, and an opposing position, with respect? For one thing, try to avoid mocking or sarcasm or name-calling. This is sometimes hard to do, because it feels *great* to get nasty about positions you don't like. (Don't you love to do it? I do!) But respectfulness is not just a matter of politeness; it's an essential step in keeping a philosophical discussion from turning into an argument. Like that guy on the opposing basketball team who elbows and pushes, a philosopher who argues dirty is a person nobody wants to play with.

> *A nasty tactic in political philosophy is calling your opponent a Nazi. A terribly irresponsible exaggeration at best. (Except when you're talking about Heidegger. At a speech at Freiburg University, where he was rector [the highest academic official], he said: "Let not propositions and 'ideas' be the rules of your being. The Führer alone is the present and future German reality and its law.... Heil Hitler!"[7])*

For another thing, when you talk or write about an opposing position, you should try your best to provide a reasonable version—as convincing as possible—of that position. (Don't hold back on this. If you provide a completely convincing version of an opposed argument that's great—you've now changed your mind about the issue, and progress has been made!) Giving a silly version of a position you're opposed to is a flaw in argumentation that's common enough to deserve its own name: it's called the fallacy of attacking (or knocking down) a "straw man."

> *Fallacies (flaws in reasoning) occur in many forms. (In what follows, we'll take a look at some more.) The odd name "straw man" here may originate from the easily knocked down scarecrow-like human figure stuffed with straw that was used for military training—a replacement for a real opponent, conveniently harmless and easily overcome. (The desire to remove gratuitously gendered terms from the*

language has resulted in the suggestion that this be renamed the "straw person.")

One fairly common way to produce a silly version of an opposing position you want to attack is to take a statement of that position out of context, or too literally, or with a meaning not really intended by those holding that position. It's tempting—I do it a bit in this book—but try not to. It's not fair, and it won't do anybody any good. Try instead to put yourself in your opponent's position, to understand sympathetically and intelligently what that person really has in mind, and what pretty good reasons that person might have for holding that position.

Yes, I know, a few philosophical positions, and arguments for them, are just plain stupid. ("There is nothing one can imagine so strange or so unbelievable that has not been said by one or other of the philosophers."—René Descartes[8]) I could tell you about some really just completely fantastically dumb positions that famous philosophers have held. (Ask me another time.) But these are rare, so you should try to think that there are some pretty good reasons for a position you encounter in a respectable context (I'm excluding what your friends say at 2 a.m. after many beers).

WHAT NOT TO IMITATE

Future philosophers tend to learn their style of argumentation by imitating their elders who are already established in the business. When I was a wee lad in graduate school, during the late Stone Age, famous philosophers came to my university to read papers. A lot of them treated philosophical argumentation as a blood sport. A couple of the worst I'll call Professors X and Y to keep them anonymous (although their real names were Max Black and Nelson Goodman). They would characteristically respond to student questions or suggestions that were critical of their positions with sarcasm and disdain, and with snotty reminders that they were famous philosophers, whereas we were mere lowly graduate students. The aim here was to leave us whimpering in the dust. You get my point by now: they should have been ashamed, not only because of this abuse of the comparatively defenceless, but also because this is argument☠, the antithesis of philosophy.

Why am I telling you this? If you're a mere student now, your totem pole position is too low to try this; but I'm just reminding you that there are some philosophical styles favoured by your elders that you should not imitate. X- and Y-style abuse has mostly disappeared (yay!). However, sometimes philosophers nowadays go overboard in reaction against all this put-down, insult, and intimidation, and instead of a gladiatorial combat till death, philosophical argumentation has become a kumbayah love-in, where everyone expresses (possibly insincere) enthusiasm over what people say when they are potentially vulnerable, and bends over backwards to be nothing but positive. Real respect for one's philosophical co-arguers is treating their positions seriously, and this can mean energetic philosophical confrontation.

COMMON(S) AD HOMINEM FALLACIES

Examples of fallacious argument technique are rare in published philosophy. But a splendidly rich source for examples is politics. So I'm going to illustrate some types of fallacies with political examples—but I'll try to add a few from philosophy.

In Canada, where I live, news broadcasts often play recorded bits from Question Period in the House of Commons. That's when politicians from a party out of power get to ask hostile questions of those in the ruling party. These questions are really argumentative assertions, but, as if they're on *Jeopardy*, they have to put them in the form of questions. The members of the government then get to reply with more hostility and endless irrelevance. We'll take a look at some invented (but not exaggerated) instances, and talk about the fallacy each illustrates.

Q: When will the government begin to recognize its responsibilities to provide adequate low-cost housing?

This is what's sometimes called a loaded or complex question. That's a question with an unjustified or controversial assumption behind it. In this case, the assumption is that the government has so far failed to recognize its responsibilities, and *any* direct answer like "right now" or "soon" or "sooner or later" or "maybe a week from Thursday" or "never" acquiesces to this assumption. Nobody is ever tricked into this response. The answer will of course be that the government already has initiated several highly successful programmes to provide what's needed. Note, however, that if, in fact, the government has not yet done anything about its responsibilities to provide such housing, then the assumption behind the question is correct, and there's nothing logically faulty about this question.

A philosophically loaded question: "Can God's existence be proven, or must we take it on faith?"

> Q: There is widespread incompetence in the Department of Correction. Why does the government continue to ignore this?
>
> A: Mr. Speaker, my honourable colleague who asked this question is notorious for his underworld connections.

The argumentative reply to the allegation of departmental incompetence is irrelevant; instead of dealing with it, the reply attacks the questioner. This sort of response is a version of what's called the *ad hominem* (Latin: "against the man") argument, which irrelevantly deals with the person making the argument or claim, instead of the content of what that person claims. The example above is a case of an *abusive* ad hominem argument.

Philosophical example of abusive ad hominem: "Nobody intelligent and mature enough to appreciate the *historicity* of St. Augustine's position would criticize it the way Prof. Martin did." (Sorry, I can't help you with this word. I never figured out what "historicity" is supposed to be.)

Here's a different variety of ad hominem argument:

> Q: How many thousands of taxpayers' dollars has the government spent on vanity advertising for its ministers?
>
> A: My honourable colleague is aware that when his party was in power, it produced a continuous stream of public-relations advertising for its members at public expense.

In this case, the reply attempts to defuse the criticism implied by the question by alleging that the questioner himself (or, in political contexts, his party) is guilty of the practice he is criticizing. This variety of *ad hominem* is called the *tu quoque* (Latin: "you too"; pronounced *too kwo-kway*). The reply in this case does nothing to counter the suggestion that a lot of public money is now being spent on such advertising; in fact, it appears to admit that. But it might tend to blunt the force of the criticism somewhat by pointing out that this is standard practice by both parties, with the implication that it's expected and accepted.

Philosophical example: "You accuse dualists like me of lack of respect for science, but I notice that your position doesn't cite any results in brain physiology research."

Another sort of ad hominem:

Q: There have been still further unconscionable, unjust, and cruel delays in the implementation of the programme of subsidies for rutabaga growers. Will the minister responsible apologize and tell us when her party will keep their promises on this?

A: It's no surprise that my honourable colleague says that, since she's trailing badly in the polls in her turnip-farming-intensive riding.

This is an example of *circumstantial ad hominem*: countering an argument or allegation by implying that the arguer's circumstances cause that person to be biased. Sometimes, of course, this sort of criticism is germane. When a policy is defended by someone on the payroll of a corporation who would benefit from that policy, that doesn't show that the policy is not a good one; but it does somewhat reduce the evidential force of that person's claims, and indicates that some further examination of the truth and fairness of those claims is probably called for.

Philosophical example: "The only reason you claim that justice requires preferential hiring for women is that it will get you a good job."

What you may have noticed about all of this is that ad hominems are really not bad reasoning, because they're not reasoning at all. They're arguments.

CHAPTER 3

WRITING PHILOSOPHY: WHY AND HOW

WHY

Writing is centrally important for philosophy—indeed, for anything involving ideas. It's more important than talking—and *much* more important than thinking. Somebody said to me long ago, "there is no such thing as thinking. There's only writing." What that person meant is that ideas don't achieve full reality until they are put into words, refined, clarified, argued for, and organized; and that can happen only in the writing process, when vague and messy half-thoughts are refined in a less vague and somewhat neater first draft, and much more in a second, third, ... *n*th draft.

The unreality of ideas just thought but not written (or spoken) is expressed by another cute saying: "How do I know what I think till I see what I write?"[9] You think you think something, but then when you talk to somebody about it, or better still, get it out on paper, it turns out to be something quite different from what you thought you thought, and better. Or else its lack of worth is revealed, and you toss it into the trash.

A source for philosophy that is even less reliable than thinking is dreaming. I once had a dream in which I wrote a whole philosophy paper. I woke up in the middle of the night just as the dream concluded, and thought, "What a great paper!", and I thought over all the details of the paper carefully so I'd remember it in the morning, and went back to sleep. When I

woke up in the morning I remembered all the details. And it
was clear to me that the whole thing was worthless nonsense.

HOW

So here comes some practical advice about how to come up with good philosophy.

Sometimes you only have a topic or a question. Don't wait till you have thought of something good to say. Sit down and start writing. Don't worry if what you write is incomplete or incoherent. You can fix that. You stand a much better chance of coming up with a good answer while you're in the process of writing. Jacques Barzun, author of more than 40 elegantly written books of history, gives this very good advice: "Convince yourself that you are working in clay, not marble, on paper not eternal bronze: let that first sentence be as stupid as it wishes."[10]

Sometimes you have thoughts about an answer to a question or, some other idea you want to communicate. STOP thinking—write.

Sometimes you get stuck: you don't know what to write next, or you reread something you wrote and realize it's not any good, or not good enough, but you don't know what to do about it. At this point, you should put your writing away, and do something as different, as mindless, as possible: watch some reruns of *Keeping Up with the Kardashians* on TV, or do something physical and strenuous, or take a nap, or drink several beers. Then—the next day is best—reread what you've written and start writing again, revising what you've got, or discarding bits of it or the whole thing, and writing more. It's much more likely that you'll know what to do after this time out.

> *Psychologists confirm that when you get stuck thinking about*
> *something you should put it away for a while; during that time,*
> *your brain is getting itself out of the dead-end grooves it had*
> *gotten into, and is putting together new approaches. While all*
> *this is happening, your conscious mind is engaged (so to speak)*
> *with Kim, Kourtney, and Khloé. It's getting your brain to work*
> *all by itself, with no attention from you. It's free brainwork!*

The only downside to this advice is that it can't be followed if you start on your philosophical project the night before it has to be finished. Should I tell you to start days or even weeks before it's due? Is there any chance you'll do that?

Here's some advice that's so important that I'll shout it at you, in all capital letters: NEVER SUBMIT A FIRST DRAFT. WHEN YOU THINK YOU'RE FINISHED, READ AND REVISE WHAT YOU'VE WRITTEN. A true wisdom-nugget: "There is no such thing as good writing. There's only good rewriting."[11] Your first draft is guaranteed NO GOOD. Reread the first draft. Rewrite it. Reread the second draft. Rewrite it. Repeat as necessary or until you can't stand to do it any more. Have I said that often enough?

CHAPTER 4

GOOD AND BAD WRITING

CLARITY

Here's a staggeringly obvious point, but one that's sometimes lost sight of: *what you write down is, on the whole, designed for reading by somebody*. At times the writer is also the expected reader, for example when you write yourself a shopping list, or keep notes in class, or write down your next dentist appointment on your calendar. But writing philosophy is (as I've been insisting) a social activity, so your philosophical writing is primarily aimed at other people. Professional philosophers write aiming at publication in a book or a journal, or at reading their work at a seminar or conference. What a student writes, on the other hand, will probably be read only by somebody who grades it, but it should be written as if—pretending that—there will be a wider audience.

Surprisingly often, writers ignore the fact that a potential (or hypothetical) audience should be able to understand what they write. You must be careful to state things very clearly, and explain things thoroughly; otherwise the audience won't understand what you're saying, or will have to struggle to figure it out. (This is not just a service to potential readers. The effort to make what you write intelligible to others will also, as I insisted above, make things more intelligible *to you*.)

But this is where a difficulty emerges. As you're writing, or when you read over what you've written, something may seem sufficiently clear and explanatory when it isn't. When you read over your writing, you (presumably) already know what you meant, but another reader is going to have to discover it on the basis of what you write. So even when your writing is clear as mud, you might think it's okay because it reminds you of what you were thinking.

The way to deal with this problem is to try to put yourself in the reader's position: keep asking yourself whether what you're writing would be clear to someone else. This is hard to do, but it's necessary.

The worth of your philosophical writing is not determined by the depth, profundity, cleverness, or originality of your thought. The best philosophical thinker in the world may nevertheless write worthless philosophy, if it doesn't communicate that thinker's great thoughts. Students who get a poor grade on a paper sometimes complain that they really understood the issues, and had some really, y'know, like, *awesome* thoughts about them, but all that just didn't come out very well in what they wrote. What they're saying may be true—nobody else is in any position to tell—but this is an irrelevant point. The worth of the writing is determined by what's written.

THE DISVALUE OF THE OBSCURE

Another important fact: PHILOSOPHICAL PROFUNDITY IS NOT COR-RELATED WITH UNITELLIGIBILITY.

 Philosophy joke.
Q: What do you get when you cross the Godfather with a philosopher?
A: An offer you can't understand.

Here are some examples you should not imitate:

> *The Einsteinian constant is not a constant, is not a centre. It is the very concept of variability—it is, finally the concept of the game. In other words, it is not the concept of something—of a centre starting from which an observer could master the field—but the very concept of the game which, after all, I was trying to elaborate.*

This famous comment on Einsteinian physics by the French philosopher Jacques Derrida has been widely passed around since he made it in a conference on his thought.[12] Many philosophers (and physicists) admit that they haven't a clue what Derrida meant. A widely circulated remark on Derrida's work is: "This kind of stuff gives bullshit a bad name."[13]

> *What is to be investigated is being only and—nothing else; being alone and further—nothing; solely being, and beyond being—nothing. What about this Nothing?...Does the Nothing exist only because the Not, i.e., the Negation, exists? Or is it the other way around? Does Negation and the Not exist only because the Nothing exists?... We assert: the Nothing is prior to the Not and the Negation.... Where do we seek the Nothing? How do we find the Nothing.... We know the Nothing.... Anxiety reveals the Nothing.... That for which and because of which we were anxious, was "really"—nothing. Indeed: the Nothing itself—as such—was present.... What about this Nothing?—The Nothing itself nothings.[14]*

> *This excerpt from Heidegger was translated, edited, and taken out of context by Rudolf Carnap, an enemy of this style of philosophical writing. Is he making it seem worse than it is? No. We should not be reluctant to accuse Heidegger of writing what can't be understood. He would probably take it as a compliment. He also wrote: "Making itself intelligible is suicide for philosophy."[15]*

Lest you think that unintelligibility is the exclusive property of dead French and German men, here's an example from the writing of Judith Butler, a distinguished (and alive) American professor at the University of California, Berkeley.

> *The move from a structuralist account in which capital is understood to structure social relations in relatively homologous ways to a view of hegemony in which power relations are subject to repetition, convergence, and rearticulation brought the question of temporality into the thinking of structure, and marked a shift from a form of Althusserian theory that takes structural totalities as theoretical objects to one in which the*

insights into the contingent possibility of structure inaugurate a renewed conception of hegemony as bound up with the contingent sites and strategies of the rearticulation of power.[16]

This one-sentence gem won first prize in the 1998 Bad Writing Contest, run by the journal *Philosophy in Literature*. If I pay very close attention to it, I think I can get a sort of inkling of what's being said, in contrast to the two preceding examples. So this one, while not totally unintelligible, is horrible in its own way: jargon-ridden, way too complex, and brutal for readers.

Writing intelligibly is not a real problem—if, that is, there's a genuine idea behind what you're trying to write. Claims that an idea is so profound and complicated that it can't be explained simply and clearly are doubtful. One suspects a desire to impress. Or maybe there's a lack of writing ability or of concern for readers. Or maybe there just wasn't a coherent idea to be communicated.

Take your time when you're writing. Don't try to squeeze too much into one sentence: write several short sentences instead of one very long one. Be as direct and simple as you can. Plain talk is always better than fancy talk.

Sometimes students can express themselves clearly in one-to-one conversation, but write gibberish. Maybe this is the result of being rewarded in high school for pretentious complex writing. Anyway, if this is your problem, try thinking about how you would talk about what you were thinking to a person standing next to you, and then write that down.

What I've been emphasizing is that philosophical talk and writing is meant to be communicated to others. Communication will not happen if they can't understand what you produce. Something else might happen of course. Because they don't understand what you're saying, people might respond, "Way cool! That's, like, so deep!" Okay, fine, if that's what you're after; but that's not doing philosophy.

JARGON

Every discipline has its own jargon. These are ordinary words used in a very narrow sense or with a new meaning, or newly coined words. There's nothing wrong with jargon. In fact, it's a necessity. When a philosopher's writing involves a new or complicated concept, one that needs a lengthy description or explanation, it's handy to refer to it using a specialized term—one that's brand new, or one that's given a new or restricted or extended meaning, or an old one that is part of the technical vocabulary philosophers understand and use. Philosophers share a large amount of jargon, and students gradually learn to understand it, at least the standard jargon in the field they're studying.

> *Students need a dictionary of philosophy jargon. A magnificently useful and inexpensive little dictionary of philosophy jargon is* The Philosopher's Dictionary, *by Robert M. Martin.*[17] *You should run to your computer, go to the Broadview Press website, and buy a copy (or two) right now. (advt.)*

It's perfectly permissible for philosophy writers to invent their own jargon to be used through the rest of a particular piece of writing, as long as this is a useful shorthand and not just a bit of annoying affectation, and as long as they provide, at first use, a very clear explanation of what those words will be used to mean.

There are several ways that jargon can be misused. Obviously, an author can be mistaken about what philosophers usually mean by an established jargon term. Or a bit of jargon might be invented where there's no need—where just saying things in ordinary English would do fine. Or, worst of all, a bit of idiosyncratic jargon—that is, jargon not part of the general philosophical vocabulary—is used without definition, or with insufficient explanation or clarification. The American physicist Steven Weinberg wondered in print what Derrida, in the quote above, might have meant by "centre," which didn't have an obvious meaning and was clearly being given a special technical sense. So he looked further into the talk by Derrida for an explanation of this word. Here's what he found:

> *Nevertheless ... structure—or rather, the structurality of structure—although it has always been involved, has always been*

*neutralized or reduced, and this by a process of giving it a centre
or referring it to a point of presence, a fixed origin.*

Weinberg says "this was not much help."[18]

EXAMPLES

These are very often an aid to explaining a position or arguing for it.
Here's an example to show how these might work.

Suppose you want to make the point that one is not morally responsible for an action (or inaction) when one is *constrained*. Nobody will
understand what you mean by that. "*Constraint*," you explain, "is the
state you're in when your actions or inactions are not the result of
your decisions, or when you would not have done otherwise had you
wanted to act differently." (This is not going to work, and I'll tell you
why later.) Maybe they still don't get it. So you give examples:

- Raoul is constrained when he fails to show up to class on
  time, because a freak ice storm shut down all the bus service,
  and that was the only way he could get to school.
- Zoe is constrained when she shoplifts because of a
  psychological compulsion: even if she had decided not to do
  it, she would have done it anyway, because of her kleptomania.
- Igor didn't hand in an assignment paper because his dog ate
  it. (Really!)
- Martha didn't break that piece of pottery on purpose. She
  dropped it because somebody bumped into her from behind.

And your argument can continue by pointing out that none of
these people are to blame for their unfortunate actions.

It's examples of this sort which turn philosophical abstractions
into something concrete. Examples are often a much clearer way
to reveal what you mean—or to prove something—than to try to
explain things in the abstract.

Examples must be chosen carefully, of course. Fleshing them out
with irrelevant details is wasting space, and can be distracting. Two
examples showing essentially the same thing is another space-waster.

Controversial or borderline cases (e.g., somebody who is alleged to be constrained to become a criminal because he was brought up in a severely dysfunctional family) may not work.

We'll have a lot more to say about the use of examples in argument (and in the particular case of the argument about moral responsibility we were just looking at) later.

GREENING

Calvin Trillin, a very famous writer of impeccable non-fiction prose, told me that the best training he had in expository writing was working on the editorial staff at *Time*, the weekly news magazine. *Time*'s reporters would send in stories, and the editorial staff would copy-edit them, checking their facts, grammar, and spelling, improving their style, and so on. A major part of the editors' job was to condense what their reporters sent in, so that it could fit into the small space it had been allotted in the next issue. In those pre-computer days, the editors worked with printed copy on paper, marking it with coloured pencils. Red pencils were used for mistake correction, and green pencils for cutting things down to fit; so the condensation process was called "greening." About this process, Trillin wrote:

> *The instructions were expressed as how many lines had to be greened—"Green seven" or "Green twelve".... I was surprised that what I had thought of as a tightly constructed seventy-line story—a story so tightly constructed that it had resisted the inclusion of that maddening leftover fact—was unharmed, or even improved, by greening ten per cent of it. The greening I did in Time Edit convinced me that just about any piece I write could be improved if, when it was supposedly ready to hand in, I looked in the mirror and said sternly to myself "Green fourteen" or "Green eight."*[19]

Try greening your writing. When you think your writing is ready to go, give it another look-through, with contraction in mind. I'm sure you will discover that sentences or even whole paragraphs can be greatly condensed or deleted, with no loss in content. Try it;

you'll be surprised that it's true. YOUR WRITING WILL BE IMPROVED TREMENDOUSLY BY SOME SEVERE GREENING. Readers are unhappy when they have to extract a comparatively small bit of content from a large pile of repetitious flabby prose. You don't want your readers to be unhappy.

AWFUL LANGUAGE

The language you use to think, speak, or write is *modular*. That means that you construct sentences not word by word, but rather out of standardized multi-word chunks. And, like modular furniture, the result is sometimes overstuffed. If you pay attention to the language you use, you can improve it considerably by eliminating the redundancy, euphemism, sloppiness, circumlocution, and just general blahblahblah that we tend to spew out by automatically combining word modules.

There are thousands of English modules that could be—should be—greened. It would be impossible to produce a list of all of them, and useless to give a very long list (because you're not going to look up everything you write on a list to see if it can be greened). I'm going to give you a sample of English modules that need greening, so that you'll get the idea. Once you're aware of this kind of problem in your writing (in *everyone's* writing!) you'll be able to fix a lot of it when you rewrite.

Okay, first comes a list of a few common overstuffed phrase modules. Notice that in each case the part that's crossed out (like ~~this~~) can be eliminated in almost every context with *zero* loss of meaning.[20]

- a few ~~short~~ years
- ~~absolutely~~ essential/necessary
- ~~any and~~ all
- ~~as far as~~ this essay ~~is concerned, it~~ will deal with
- ~~at a~~ later ~~date~~
- because ~~of the following reasons~~

- bond/collect/connect/join/mix ~~together~~
- ~~completely~~ engulf/destroy/eliminate/fill
- ~~conclusive~~ proof
- ~~diametrically~~ opposed
- each ~~and every~~
- eliminate ~~altogether/entirely~~

- ~~end~~ result
- every ~~last~~ one
- every ~~single~~ person
- ~~exact~~ same
- few ~~in number~~
- ~~final~~ conclusion/outcome
- for ~~the purpose of~~
- in ~~actual~~ fact
- ~~literally~~ true
- ~~on a~~ daily ~~basis~~

- ~~personal~~ opinion
- ~~personally,~~ I think
- pick ~~and choose~~
- ~~polar~~ opposites
- reason ~~why~~
- repeat ~~again~~
- ~~specific~~ details
- ~~theoretically~~ possible
- ~~ultimate~~ goal
- visible ~~to the eye~~

Next is a sample of bloated phrases; each can and should be replaced with the shorter (or clearer) item to its right.

a majority of	most
a negative attitude	critical? pessimistic?
address an issue	deal with? talk about? a problem
aspect	part
at this moment in time at this particular point in time at the present time	now
challenge issue	problem
concerning with regard to as regards regarding in relation to relating to with reference to with respect to pertaining to	about
dialogue with	discuss with

due to the fact that in view of the fact that	since, because
during the period that	when, while
few and far between	rare
have the capability to is capable of	can
in all probability	probably
in any way, shape, or form	at all
in the event eventuality that	if
in the majority of cases	in most cases
in the very near future	soon
indicate	say
individual	person
is much the same as	is like
it goes without saying that	obviously
it is likely that	probably
on a case-by-case basis	individually
on a regular basis	regularly
on the face of the earth	anywhere
owing to	because of
presently	soon? or now?
previous to prior to	before
subsequent to	after
the fact of the matter is that	in fact
this day and age	nowadays
time and time again	repeatedly
transpire	happen
virtually	almost

And finally, in this section, I want to warn you about some other frequent problems with expository writing.

1. Sentence Overload

Have a look at this paragraph, from the *New York Times*:

> CARACAS, Venezuela—*This country's small Jewish community was already on edge when vandals painted anti-Semitic epithets on the walls of Jewish institutions and businesses last month after President Hugo Chávez cut ties with Israel and called on Jews here to support his description of Israel's leaders as a "government of assassins."* [21]

I'll bet you had to read that more than once, and maybe didn't understand it even after a couple of tries. Can you figure out the sequence of the events mentioned? The problem here is not wordy modules, but cramming too much into one sentence. It should have been broken down into maybe three short sentences, with sequence-indicating adverbs (e.g., 'then').

2. Officialese

Some awful language results from the speaker's desire to appear more learned or knowledgeable or official. The thought is that this would impress people, and that straightforward clear and plain language would not. A police constable I heard interviewed on a radio news broadcast emitted this sentence: "The other police officer and myself observed an individual exiting from their vehicle," when what he meant was, I guess, that he and his partner saw someone get out of a car. Are you impressed by how professional this guy is? Do you really think your audience would be impressed by this kind of officialese in your talk or writing? Trust me: they won't.

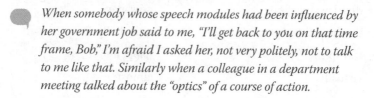

When somebody whose speech modules had been influenced by her government job said to me, "I'll get back to you on that time frame, Bob," I'm afraid I asked her, not very politely, not to talk to me like that. Similarly when a colleague in a department meeting talked about the "optics" of a course of action.

3. Timidity

Authors say:

> "*I feel that [X]*"
> "*I think that [X]*"
> "*From my point of view, [X]*"
> "*In my opinion, [X]*,"

instead of just asserting that [X]. Or they will waffle about assertions in other ways: "Plato seems to argue that [X]" when what they really mean is that Plato *does* argue that [X]. Sometimes, of course, it really is appropriate to weaken one's assertions with this sort of softening; but if you're really so unsure about a great deal of what you're asserting in a paper, you should go back and study things more first, to get some firmer opinions. Philosophical expository writing, after all, *is supposed to make some claims*. But I suspect that this sort of thing is really not a sign that the author is unsure, but rather a way of being nice, as if making a straight-out assertion is somehow aggressive. It isn't, really.

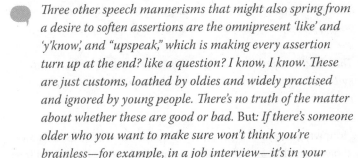

> *Three other speech mannerisms that might also spring from a desire to soften assertions are the omnipresent 'like' and 'y'know', and "upspeak," which is making every assertion turn up at the end? like a question? I know, I know. These are just customs, loathed by oldies and widely practised and ignored by young people. There's no truth of the matter about whether these are good or bad. But: If there's someone older who you want to make sure won't think you're brainless—for example, in a job interview—it's in your interest to try to avoid these verbal tics. And something else to avoid: the frequent injection of the word 'basically'.*

4. The Missing "I"

But there is also underuse of 'I' and 'my'. Did you learn that these words are banned from academic writing? Instead of 'I' people were sometimes told to substitute 'the present author'. Why was that supposed to be an improvement?

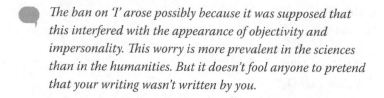

The ban on 'I' arose possibly because it was supposed that this interfered with the appearance of objectivity and impersonality. This worry is more prevalent in the sciences than in the humanities. But it doesn't fool anyone to pretend that your writing wasn't written by you.

Another substitute is 'we', which is outdated, even if you're the Queen of England, and makes for absurdity, as in "A few days ago, we asked our husband whether...."

The old-fashioned rule is to avoid 'I' is disappearing, especially in the humanities, but do check with your teacher to see what's expected.

5. Too Much Passivity

Overuse of the passive voice makes ponderous prose. Do they still teach you about the active/passive voice distinction in school? If not you'll figure it out by considering the difference between the passive construction in the left column, and the better (simpler, clearer, more natural, easier to read) active construction in the right:

Metaphysical dualism has been argued for by philosophers for centuries.	*Philosophers have been arguing for metaphysical dualism for centuries.*
That God is capable of doing evil has long been denied by theists.	*Theists have long denied that God is capable of doing evil.*

The following example from a real-life paper avoids 'I', uses an awkward passive voice, and generally overstuffs. Look at how awful it is:

In a recent paper by the present author a simple practical procedure of predictor identification has been proposed. It is the purpose of this paper to provide a theoretical and empirical basis of the procedure.[22]

Compare this rewrite:

I proposed, in a recent paper, a simple practical procedure of pre-dictor identification. Here I provide a theoretical and empirical basis of the procedure.

Don't you feel better when you read the rewrite?

DO AS I SAY NOT AS I DO

You might recall that the subject of this book was how to do philosophy. But the book wandered off into advice on what makes for good philosophical writing, or good expository writing in general. Well, yes, but I hope that what we've wandered into is of use to you anyway. But do bear in mind that when you write a real philosophy paper or book (and not a wandering chat like this one), that getting off the main point is a defect.

One way the first draft of what you write will be terrible is that it will be disorganized—wandering all over the place. If you're doing things right, this is inevitable. In your first draft, you will (and should) try different approaches, repeat yourself, change your mind, forget what the point you're trying to make is, and so on. So (have I mentioned this earlier?) one or more revisions are necessary. As you revise, you'll figure out what you're aiming at doing, and how you're going to get there; and you can sort things out into a logical order.

 Imagine how much more difficult this was to do in Ancient Times, without word-processor cut-and-paste. Sometimes we resorted to literal scissors and literal paste.

Keep reminding yourself what the topic of your writing is. Reorganize or cut when you've wandered. Pay attention to the overall structure of your work, and be clear in your own mind where you're heading.

A nicely organized paper lets readers know what's going on. Student papers sometimes fail to give the reader any idea of where they're heading and how they're going to get there. Once you get clear on what the structure of your paper is, make sure you make this clear to the reader. One way to do this nicely is by having labelled sections to your paper:

Part 1: The Question
Part 2: X's Answer
Part 3: What's Wrong with X's Answer
Part 4: My Answer.

Maybe in high school they told you to make the overall plan of what you write clear by first saying what you're going to say, then saying it, then saying what you just said. No no, please no. That's too much. Take pity on your paper's markers: after reading this useless routine in several papers, they'll be screaming, to release the pressure inside their heads, and reaching for something illegal to smoke. What's needed here is a balance between leaving the reader totally lost, and annoying the reader with all that ritual over-signposting.

CHAPTER 5

HOW ARGUMENTS WORK

S o far, we've been talking about arguments as interactions. But now we're going to shift gears slightly, and look at arguments from a more traditional perspective: as things produced, without much reference to where these things are aimed, and how they function interpersonally. This is the perspective from which logicians have traditionally categorized and evaluated various kinds of arguments. This sort of examination, it's hoped, will make your arguments better no matter where they're aimed.

We'll start with some basic ideas about the structure of arguments. They are standard bits of philosophical lore, and as a philosopher you're expected to know about them. See if they're helpful.

THE BASIC STRUCTURES

It's standard to distinguish the *conclusion* of an argument, and its *premises*. 'Premises' is plural, and the usual singular is 'premise'. (An infrequent, older, but still acceptable spelling for the singular form is 'premiss'.) Supporting the conclusion—establishing its truth, or making it more probable—is the aim of argument; and the premises are statements brought to support the conclusion. (Another way of saying that premises support a conclusion is to say that they *imply* the conclusion. Be careful about using the words 'imply' and 'infer'. Premises *imply* a conclusion; someone *infers* a conclusion from premises.)

Supporting a conclusion is different from merely asserting it (no matter how emphatically). Arguing against a conclusion is different from merely denying it.

Monty Python's elucidation:
Client: ... *Look this isn't an argument.*
Mr. Vibrating: *Yes it is.*
Client: *No it isn't, it's just contradiction.*
Mr. Vibrating: *No it isn't.*
Client: *It is. You just contradicted me.*
Mr. Vibrating: *No I didn't.*
Client: *I came here for a good argument.*
Mr. Vibrating: *No you didn't, you came here for an argument.*
Client: *Well, an argument's not the same as contradiction.*
Mr. Vibrating: *It can be.*
Client: *No it can't. An argument is a connected series of*
statements to establish a definite proposition.
Mr. Vibrating: *No it isn't.*
Client: *Yes it is.*[23]

The following old clichéd argument has two premises and a conclusion.

All men are mortal.	(First premise)
Socrates is a man.	(Second premise)
Therefore Socrates is mortal.	(Conclusion)

The word 'therefore' identifies the conclusion here, but arguments don't have to have that word. It's clear which statement is the conclusion if it says "So Socrates is mortal," or "It follows that Socrates is mortal." And the conclusion doesn't have to come last. This is the same argument: "Socrates is mortal, because all men are mortal and Socrates is a man." You might even leave out those words that indicate conclusion or premises, if it's clear what's supposed to be supported by what.

There are two requirements that must be satisfied in any good argument: the premises must be true, and they must support the conclusion. That Socrates-argument is a good one: the two premises are true, and the conclusion follows—that is, it's supported by those premises. Note that when I say that it's a good argument, I don't mean that it's informative or interesting or useful or anything like that. This boring old argument has none of those characteristics, but it's a good one.

This one isn't any good:

No pigs can fly.
All pigs are mammals.
Therefore some mammals can fly.

Both of the premises are true, but they don't support the conclusion. The conclusion is true (bats!), but that's irrelevant—it doesn't make this argument any better. The premises are true, but for this argument to be a good one, they have to support the conclusion, and these don't. What the premises say doesn't make the conclusion any more believable. Compare this one:

No pigs can fly.
All pigs are mammals.
Therefore no mammals can fly.

A false conclusion this time, but again unsupported by the premises. This one isn't any good:

All pigs can fly.
Anything that can fly is lighter than air.
Therefore all pigs are lighter than air.

These premises *do* support the conclusion. Do you see what's meant by "support the conclusion" here? It means that *if* those premises were true, *then* the conclusion would be true also. But the argument isn't good because of false premises.
Compare this argument:

All pigs are mammals.
All mammals oink.
Therefore all pigs oink.

Again, the premises support the conclusion. If they were true, then the conclusion would be true. But they have to *all* be true for the argument to be a good one. I'm a real expert when it comes to

zoology, so you can trust me when I tell you that the first premise is true but the second one is false. So again this is not a good
argument.

Is this a good argument?

Christmas day always falls on the same day of the week as the
following New Year's day.
Christmas day 2030 falls on a Wednesday.
So New Year's Day 2031 falls on a Wednesday.

The premises do support the conclusion: you can see that if those
two premises are true, then the conclusion would have to be true
also. Are those premises true? You may already realize that the first
one is true, but you probably don't know whether the second one is
or not. You can tell that the premises support the conclusion even if
you don't know whether the premises are true or not. (They're true.
So it's a good argument.)

This argument is pretty good:

It has snowed every winter in Halifax for centuries.
So it will snow there next winter.

The premise is true and it does make the conclusion *very likely*, but
the truth of the premise (only one in this case) doesn't guarantee the
truth of the conclusion. Notice the difference between this argument
and the previous ones, in which either the premises support the conclusion or they don't. It's a matter of yes or no. Here it's a question
about the *degree* to which the premise supports the conclusion. This
premise supports the conclusion to a very high degree. We'll talk
more about this difference in the next section.

Many dogs climb trees.
So Snookums, the Schmidlap's pit bull terrier, might be found up
in the branches of the tree in their backyard.

Here we also have a fair degree of support for the conclusion, rather
less than in the snow example. The argument isn't any good at all,

however, because the premise, of course, is false (though a few dogs actually can climb trees—Google for videos).

This argument isn't much good:

> In the majority of recent cases, the taller of the two leading
> US presidential candidates won.
> Therefore in the 2024 election, if they're not the same height,
> the taller of the two leading US presidential candidates
> will win.

The premise is true (but not by much: 18 out of 28 winners between 1900 and 2011 have been taller), and we might suppose it gives some support to the idea that there's maybe some connection between height and winning, and thus to the conclusion. But it's not enough support to give the conclusion much believability, not really enough for most purposes. I wouldn't use this argument as a basis for betting any meaningful amount of money on the 2024 election.

This argument, which no doubt you've heard a version of from a smoking relative, is worthless:

> Uncle Max smoked two packs of cigarettes a day his whole adult
> life, and he lived to 99.
> Grandma Betty smoked like a chimney starting at age 15, and
> she was never sick a day in her life.
> Therefore cigarettes aren't a health hazard.

The premises may be true, but they provide really vanishingly small support to the conclusion—next to none. A sample of two is far too small to justify that sweeping conclusion. A much larger sample, better collected in various ways, would be needed.

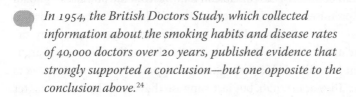

In 1954, the British Doctors Study, which collected information about the smoking habits and disease rates of 40,000 doctors over 20 years, published evidence that strongly supported a conclusion—but one opposite to the conclusion above.[24]

DEDUCTION

Here's maybe something you learned: There are two kinds of arguments, deductive and inductive. Deductive arguments are ones that go from the general to the particular (or specific), and inductive go from the particular/specific to the general. That's right, isn't it?

No. That way of distinguishing inductive and deductive arguments was rejected by logicians over a century ago, though it still hangs on here and there. (Google "deductive inductive general particular specific" to find over 553,000 examples. Why are people still saying this?)

Here's the distinction between the two kinds of arguments that has replaced that one. A deductive argument constructed correctly—philosophers call it a *valid* deductive argument—is one in which if the premises are true, then the conclusion *has to be* true. In other words, it's *impossible* that the premises were true but the conclusion false. (Remember, please, that this is not all it takes to be a good deductive argument. In addition, the premises have to be true.) Here are two valid deductive arguments:

> The countries on the Iberian Peninsula are Spain and Portugal.
> Spain grows olives.
> Portugal grows olives.
> Therefore all the countries on the Iberian Peninsula grow olives.

> All vegetables are poisonous.
> Everything poisonous is green.
> Therefore all vegetables are green.

Satisfy yourself that both arguments are valid. All the statements in the first are true; but that isn't relevant to its validity. Everything is false in the second, and that's not relevant either. What's relevant is that in both cases the conclusion follows from the premises—should the premises be true, the conclusion would have to be true also. It would be a self-contradiction to assert the premises and deny the conclusion. That's what makes it valid. To see that the second argument is a valid deductive argument, *suppose* the two premises were true. They aren't, duh, but just suppose they were. Then, as a matter of logic, the conclusion would have to be true. Again, it would be a self-contradiction to assert the premises but deny the conclusion. In each case, it would be impossible that the premises were true, but the conclusion false.

The only way the actual truth or falsity of premises and conclusion can be relevant to its validity is when the premises are all in fact true, and the conclusion is in fact false. Then you know that the argument is invalid. (That situation is impossible in a valid argument, right?)

Here's an invalid deductive argument:

If Arnold hasn't eaten, then he's hungry.
Arnold is hungry.
Therefore he hasn't eaten.

You don't know anything about Arnold, so you don't know whether any of these statements are true or false. What you do know, however, is that it's possible for those two premises to be true while the conclusion is false. We can imagine a state of affairs in which this is the case. Imagine that Arnold has just eaten, but that he is hungry all the time—when he hasn't eaten, and when he has. So the premises are both true, but the conclusion is false. The fact that we can imagine a consistent state of affairs in which the premises are both true and the conclusion is false shows that the truth of both premises is consistent with the falsity of the conclusion. Thus it shows that the argument is invalid.

Here's another invalid argument:

All the students in my logic class own the logic book.
Shawn owns the logic book.
Therefore Shawn is a student in my logic class.

Imagine a state of affairs to show this argument is invalid.

INDUCTION

Inductive arguments, on the other hand, are all invalid. The truth of the premises of a strong inductive argument doesn't *guarantee* the truth of the conclusion. It's possible, given true premises, to have a false conclusion. One might assert the premises and deny the conclusion without self-contradiction. True premises would, however, make the conclusion *more likely*, to some degree. Call that degree the *strength* of the argument.

It would seem, then, that true-premise deductive arguments, which guarantee a true conclusion, are much better than true-premise inductive arguments, which only make the conclusion more probable. The problem is that often an inductive argument is the best you can get. (Think about the smoking/health argument in the *British Medical Journal,* talked about above. You can't get a deductive argument that smoking is bad for everyone past, present, and future. But that very big sample gives very strong evidence for that conclusion, and that's plenty good enough.)

We've seen some examples of inductive arguments with varying degrees of strength. Here are some fairly strong ones:

Mom has phoned me every Sunday night for the past year.
Therefore Mom will phone me this coming Sunday night.

Professor Plum was murdered.
Professor Plum's blood is all over Miss Peacock's gloves.
Therefore Miss Peacock was the murderer.

People who have studied philosophy almost invariably have a
    great sense of humour.
Steve Martin was a philosophy student.
Therefore Steve Martin has a great sense of humour.

You can see how the truth of the premise would make the truth of the conclusion more likely, but that it's still possible that the premise(s) be true but the conclusion false. (In the first one, because Mom's telephone is broken, or she's suddenly developed other interests, etc. In the second one because it was in fact Col. Mustard who murdered Professor Plum—he did it with an axe in the drawing room, and then wiped his axe off on Miss Peacock's gloves. In the third one, because a premise says "almost." If that were true, and given the truth of the other premise, it would still be possible that in this particular case, it didn't turn out that way.)

The conclusion of the third argument is true. That doesn't make it a good argument. Its conclusion is strongly supported by its premises, but one of the premises is not true.

> *Steve Martin was in fact a philosophy student in university. (Score one for us!) The first premise isn't true. You probably know a number of philosophy-trained people with zero sense of humour, possibly because they're not bright enough, or take themselves too seriously. On the other hand, philosophy scores comparatively well for humour. I once heard a radio interview with a sociologist who had been studying academic jokes (no kidding). He reported that philosophers had more jokes about their discipline than any other academic specialty. But what makes the first premise false is that 'almost invariably' is too strong.*

But notice again—this bears repeating so don't get annoyed—that the strength of an inductive argument is a matter of how likely the conclusion would be given the truth of the premises. It has nothing to do with whether the premises are in fact true. You can evaluate the strength of these inductive arguments without knowing anything about the truth of these premises (does Mom phone or not? What are the known facts about the Plum murder case?), and you can find an argument inductively strong even though you know that it's not the case that all the premises are true (as in the case of the third argument).

As you've noticed, with inductive arguments, support of the conclusion is not all-or-nothing. It's a matter of degree. That's why the sample inductive arguments above were rated as very strong, or pretty strong, or not strong at all. How strong is strong enough? That depends on the situation: some situations require more confidence in the conclusion than others. The relevant considerations are how much it costs to be wrong, and how much benefit would come from being right. For example, when the TV weather forecaster predicts rain, that's fairly good evidence—good enough to make it reasonable for you to take your umbrella—because if it's wrong, that's no big deal. That argument about smoking above is so weak, and the consequences of believing its conclusion, if it's false, are so important, that it's clear that your Uncle Harry, who believes that conclusion on the basis of that evidence, is shown to be, um, not terribly bright. The evidence needed to convict someone of murder needs to be very strong. Sometimes there is some pretty strong inductive evidence for the defendant's guilt, but the jury decides that the evidence isn't strong enough to convict; but later, that defendant loses when he is sued for damages for causing a "wrongful death," on the basis of more or less the same evidence. There's no contradiction there; trials for criminal charges (e.g., murder) need very strong evidence to convict (evidence that makes the defendant's guilt "beyond reasonable doubt"); but civil suits need evidence that's not that strong (evidence that shows the complainant's charge is merely more probably true than the defendant's).

 A real life (and famous) example: O.J. Simpson's 1995 trial found the evidence insufficient to convict him of a double murder, but in 1997 he was successfully sued for causing the wrongful death of one of the victims (and for battery of the other).

In case you're getting confused about terminology, here's a summary.

A *good deductive* argument:
- Has only true premises
   and
- Is *valid*; that is, the truth of the premises would necessitate— guarantee—the truth of the conclusion.

A *bad deductive* argument:
- Has one or more false premises
   and/or
- Is *invalid*; that is, the truth of the premises would be consistent with the falsity of the conclusion.

A *good inductive* argument:
- Has only true premises
   and

- Is *strong* (enough); that is, the truth of the premises would make the conclusion acceptably likely.

A *bad inductive* argument:
- Has one or more false premises
  and/or
- Is *insufficiently strong*; that is, the truth of the premises would not make the conclusion acceptably likely.

Now, by the way, we can see where that slogan about particular and general goes wrong. That argument about the Iberian Peninsula:

The countries on the Iberian Peninsula are Spain and Portugal.
Spain grows olives.
Portugal grows olives.
Therefore all the countries on the Iberian Peninsula grow olives.

goes from the particular to the general, but it's deductive. And that argument about Mom phoning:

Mom has phoned me every Sunday night for the past year.
Therefore Mom will phone me this coming Sunday night.

goes from the general to the particular, but it's inductive. There's no useful distinction between arguments involving going particular-to-general or general-to-particular, and that's why logicians don't talk about that any longer. So if you learned that particular/general distinction, fuhgeddaboudit.

Logicians beginning with Aristotle (fourth century BCE) have been working toward general theories about what makes conclusions follow from premises, for valid deductive and strong inductive arguments. (There's been a lot of progress since then; that particular/general business is a leftover from the Aristotelian tradition.) We're not going to go into general theory here. Instead, we're going to talk about particular kinds of arguments, especially those often found in philosophy, with some hints about how to distinguish good and bad ones.

CHAPTER 6

"THAT'S LIKE ARGUING"

Whether or not the premises support the conclusion of a deductive argument—that is, whether or not it's valid— is not a matter of the particular assertions in that argument, but of the argument's *logical form*. What exactly logical form is, is a complicated matter we're not going to go into here, but you'll get the idea from some examples. We can show that a proposed deductive argument is invalid by producing a second argument, parallel to the first, with the same logical form but different premises and conclusion—premises that are clearly true, and a conclusion that's clearly false. This is what we're calling the "that's like arguing" objection.

> *The* LSAT *(Law School Admission Test) contains questions giving a bit of reasoning, and asking which of the multiple choices has the same logical form. There are lots of websites intended to help you prepare for the* LSAT *by giving examples of this sort of question and advice on how to figure out the answers. To find the "that's-like-arguing" technique: Google its official name:* parallel reasoning.

Some examples:

If Arnold hasn't eaten, then he's hungry.
Arnold is hungry.
Therefore he hasn't eaten.

This is the deductively invalid argument we encountered above. That's like arguing:

> If the population of Chicago is more than 30 million, then it's bigger than Moose Jaw.
> Chicago is bigger than Moose Jaw.
> Therefore the population of Chicago is more than 30 million.

(Population estimates, 2012: Chicago 2,713,000; Moose Jaw 35,500.) Both of these arguments have the same logical form, which we can indicate this way:

> If *A* then *B*
> *B*
> Therefore *A*.

The second one clearly has true premises and a false conclusion. This shows that all arguments with that logical form are invalid.

Another invalid argument is this one, presented above:

> All the students in my logic class own the logic book.
> Shawn owns the logic book.
> Therefore Shawn is a student in my logic class.

That's like arguing:

> All the South Pacific islands have palm trees.
> Florida has palm trees.
> Therefore Florida is a South Pacific Island.

The invalid logical form of both is

> All *A*s are *B*s
> *X* is a *B*
> Therefore *X* is an *A*.

"THAT'S LIKE ARGUING": CRITIQUING OTHER KINDS OF ARGUMENTS

Well, remember that all inductive arguments are invalid, so all of them will fail the "that's like arguing" test as outlined above. This is an example of a good inductive argument:

> Lucas Giolito is a rookie pitcher for a National League baseball club (the Washington Nationals).
> National League pitchers these days almost invariably have a season batting average less than .250.
> Therefore we can expect Giolito to have a season batting average this year of less than .250.

The argument has the logical form

> *A* is a *B*
> *B*s almost invariably are *C*
> Therefore *A* is a *C*,

and we can create an argument of that form with true premises and a false conclusion:

> Duck-billed platypuses are mammals.
> Mammals almost invariably bear live young.
> Therefore duck-billed platypuses bear live young.

During the 2015 season, National League pitchers had a miserable cumulative batting average of .131. Of the 143 pitchers who had any at-bats during the season, only 12 had an average greater than .250. Giolito's batting record in the minors, by the way, doesn't show anything. During those five seasons, he pitched in 57 games, and had a batting average of .000, but then he only had three at-bats (plus two sacrifice bunts).

And, in unrelated news: the platypus and four species of spiny anteaters, all mammals, lay eggs.

The Giolito and platypus arguments are deductively invalid. Nevertheless, considered as inductive arguments, they can be pretty strong. The one about pitchers does make its conclusion pretty likely. The one about platypuses, with a false conclusion, is also a strong inductive argument. The conclusion is made likely by those premises. (Platypuses are weird—unlikely—mammals.) Note carefully here: when evaluating the strength of the platypus argument, you shouldn't consider whether that conclusion is true or false. Even though it's false, the truth of those two premises make the conclusion quite probably true. If those premises were all you knew about the facts, it would be reasonable for you to think that the conclusion was true.

So what would show that an inductive argument is no good is not that there couldn't be one of that form with true premises and a false conclusion, but rather that those kinds of premises don't, in fact, make the conclusion probable (or probable enough). So when we produce a "that's like arguing" counter-argument for a proposed inductive argument, what's needed is a set of premises that—very roughly speaking—reports facts that are supposed to make the conclusion probable in the same way as in the purported argument, but where the conclusion isn't probable. That description probably didn't mean very much to you. Giving a clear account of what makes for a good inductive argument is a difficult task indeed. Instead, and better, I'm going to give some examples of successful "that's like arguing" criticisms of inductive arguments.

In each of the following cases, the target argument will be followed with a parallel argument, labelled TLA (for "that's like arguing"), which uses the same type of facts that are supposed to make the conclusion sufficiently probable, but in the parallel argument, clearly do not. Then there will be some commentary on good and bad arguments of that type. I'll give you the official names of the mistakes in reasoning here, where there is an official name, in case this will ever be of any help to you.

You'll find that just about all heroin users smoked marijuana when they were much younger. Therefore marijuana use is dangerous.

The TLA argument:

> *Just about all mass murderers drank milk when they were much younger. Therefore drinking milk is dangerous.*

What's behind the reasoning in the target argument is the supposition that if X usually comes before Y, it's probable that X causes Y. But there are plenty of examples in which X usually comes before Y, but does not cause Y, and the TLA argument gives a clear one. Because there are many examples of this, X coming before Y does not make it probable that X causes Y. This bad reasoning happens frequently enough to merit an official name (and you can't get more official than saying something in Latin): it's *post hoc ergo propter hoc*, meaning, "after this, therefore because of this."

However, you should note that if there's really a very consistent history of Xs preceding Ys, that's some inductive evidence that X does have some sort of causal relation with Y. (Maybe, for example, Xs and Ys both are caused by something else.) A good question we won't answer here: what evidence do you need in addition to make it more likely—likely enough—that Xs cause Ys?[25]

Here are four examples from philosophy of a different sort of what appears to be mistaken reasoning.

> *"No fact can be real or existent, no statement true, unless there be a sufficient reason why it is so and not otherwise." So the "sequence of things diffused through the universe of created objects" must have a sufficient reason also. Leibniz uses this reasoning to conclude that there must exist a non-contingent being—a necessary being, God—who is the sufficient reason for the whole universe of created (contingent) beings.*[26]

> *Atoms aren't conscious. Brains are physical things, nothing but atoms. Therefore brains aren't conscious.*

> *"Should we not assume that just as the eye, hand, the foot, and in general each part of the body clearly has its own proper function, so man too has some function over and above the function*

of his parts?"[27] *This is bad reasoning if Aristotle is arguing to the conclusion that humans have functions from the premise that their parts have functions. But maybe this is just an analogy—just the claim that humans have functions just as their parts do.*

We see that every city-state is a community of some sort, and that every community is established for the sake of some good (for everyone performs every action for the sake of what he takes to be good).[28]

All three of these can be criticized by this TLA argument:

Each individual potato in this bag weighs under a pound. Therefore the whole bag of potatoes weighs under a pound.

Sometimes, but not always, the fact that each item in a collection has a property implies that the whole collection has that property. The fact that each of the nine buildings that make up Chattahoochee Valley Community College (Go Pirates!) is located in Phenix City, Alabama, does imply (and not make it merely more likely) that Chattahoochee Valley Community College is itself located in Phenix City, Alabama. But in a good proportion of cases, you can't draw that sort of conclusion. The mistaken use of that inference has an official name: *the fallacy of composition.* There's also the converse mistaken sort of reasoning: because a whole thing has a certain property, therefore each of its parts do. That's called the *fallacy of division*:

Birds are common in North America.
Starlings are birds.
Therefore starlings are common in North America.

Premises and conclusion are true here, but you hardly need a TLA counter-argument to see the obvious fault in this argument. We could provide a TLA argument to show that this is no good:

Birds are common in North America.
Penguins are birds.
Therefore penguins are common in North America.

But this is not worth the effort. In fact, it's very hard to find any examples, in philosophy or in everyday reasoning, of either division or composition, that would fool anyone.

Clear real-life examples of these two fallacies in philosophy are very rare. After an energetic search, I've found only those four examples that might be the fallacy of composition, and none of division, in philosophy. Writers engaged in the critical-thinking industry claim that both these fallacies infect everyday argumentation, but my search of their examples turned up only two or three that are sort-of realistic, and are arguably not cases of these fallacies at all; and hundreds of silly arguments that nobody would take seriously. You might well wonder why they (and some of the other classical fallacies) are taken to be important. The answer is probably that talking about them is traditional. Aristotle categorized these (and 11 others) in his Sophistical Refutations *(Sophistici Elenchi), and, as we've seen, the Aristotelian logical tradition remains strong.*

A different reasoning problem:

We shouldn't allow euthanasia for terminally ill patients in great pain. If that were allowed, it would lead to legalization of killing of people who are very depressed or just very inconvenient.

The TLA argument:

TLA: You shouldn't play solitaire on your computer. This will lead to your getting addicted to compulsive Internet gaming, and your life will be ruined.

This sort of argument occasionally has a point: when there is a significant risk that one thing will lead to a series of events, and eventually to something definitely bad. But that has to be likely for this argument to work, and it's almost always up to the person giving this argument to provide some good reason to think that this series of events would result. This sort of argument is called the "slippery slope argument," whether or not the slope to the alleged result is in fact slippery.

The next example resembles a slippery slope, but isn't the same:

> *You shouldn't walk on the grass, because if everyone did that, all that nice grass would die.*

The TLA argument:

> *You shouldn't walk across that bridge, because if everyone did that, the enormous weight would make the bridge collapse.*

It's not a slippery slope because it's not implied here that the initial instance(s) of this will lead to more. This is a very interesting sort of argument, and it appears that the walking on the grass argument may not be a mistake in moral reasoning at all. Two questions arise: When is it morally relevant to imagine what would result if everyone did that? and Why is it ever relevant, given that your doing it is not going to *result in* everyone's doing it? I'm not even going to begin to talk about these issues.

Another reasoning problem:

> *You can't prove that God doesn't exist. Therefore nobody is entitled to doubt it.*

The TLA argument:

> *If I were to suggest that between the Earth and Mars there is a china teapot revolving about the sun in an elliptical orbit, nobody would be able to disprove my assertion provided I were careful to add that the teapot is too small to be revealed even by our*

most powerful telescopes. But if I were to go on to say that, since my assertion cannot be disproved, it is an intolerable presumption on the part of human reason to doubt it, I should rightly be thought to be talking nonsense.

I'm quoting Bertrand Russell. He goes on to say: "If, however, the existence of such a teapot were affirmed in ancient books, taught as the sacred truth every Sunday, and instilled into the minds of children at school, hesitation to believe in its existence would become a mark of eccentricity and entitle the doubter to the attentions of the psychiatrist in an enlightened age or of the Inquisitor in an earlier time."

 These quotations are from an article entitled "Is There a God?," an article commissioned by Illustrated Magazine, *but never published, presumably because Russell's critique of the reasoning of some religious people would have offended many readers.*

The premise stating that you can't disprove the existence of God is, by the way, often produced by defenders of religious belief.[29] The question is what follows from it.

What's at issue here is the *burden of proof*. To say that one side of a disagreement has the burden of proof is to say that that side needs to present evidence or argument, but the other side does not. The clearest cases are those in which the burden of proof is on the proponent of a new or surprising idea, one that goes against common sense or accepted science or conventional wisdom. It's also clear where this burden lies when one side has presented some pretty good evidence for its position; then it's up to the other side to respond. Russell's teapot hypothesis clearly is the sort of idea that bears the burden of proof, but the idea that God exists doesn't appear (at least to believers) to bear that burden, because it's hardly new or surprising, or contrary to what many take to be common sense. If, as supposed, there's no evidence against that idea, then it would appear that the unbeliever has the burden of proof. But on the other hand, it does seem to be a mistake, in this case, to assign the total burden to the atheist, and to conclude, if the atheist fails to provide sufficient contrary evidence, that we can take God's existence for granted. Maybe the best response in this particular case is to say that if there really is no sufficient reasoning in support of either side, then neither can be taken for granted. Or maybe there is an asymmetry of burden of proof here, because existence claims of something unobservable are easy to make, but sometimes very difficult or impossible to disprove

Here's another TLA response to an argument sometimes heard in religious circles:

> *It is often argued that religion is valuable because it makes men good.*

The TLA argument:

> *But even if this were true it would not be a proof that religion is true. Santa Claus makes children good in precisely the same way, and yet no one would argue seriously that the fact proves his existence.*[30]

CHAPTER 7

WHERE YOU GET TRUE PREMISES: THE OBVIOUS

TRUE/JUSTIFIED PREMISES

A good argument satisfies two requirements: the premises are true; and the premises support the conclusion. So criticism of an argument often involves questioning of the truth of the premises. Let's take a look at an example. Here's a well-known philosophical argument against the idea that the actions of human beings are, like the behaviour of other familiar objects, determined by causes.

> Premise (1): Human beings are sometimes responsible for their actions.
>
> Premise (2): You're responsible for an action only if you could have done otherwise.
>
> Premise (3): You could have done otherwise only if pre-existent causes did not determine your action.
>
> Conclusion: Sometimes human actions are not determined by pre-existent causes.

"Responsibility" here means *agency*—the person responsible for an action *did it* (contrasted with: *it happened to* that person). Think of causation by pre-existent causes in terms of how throwing a switch causes a light bulb to go on: throwing that switch, together with other conditions already in place (current in the wires, wires in circuit all connected, switch in working order, light bulb working and screwed in properly) determines that the light goes on.

Okay, so let's consider whether the conclusion here is supported. First, does the conclusion follow from the premises? This is not an extremely simple argument like the ones we've been looking at, because the logical words 'only if' tend to confuse some people, but think of it this way. The first premise says that there are instances of responsible human action; together with the second premise, that implies that there are actions that could have been done otherwise. This subconclusion together with the third premise implies that those actions are not determined by pre-existent causes; the conclusion that some human actions are not thus determined follows. The logic is fine. In fact, this is a valid deductive argument.

To the extent that any of those premises is open to significant doubt, support is removed from the conclusion. The question then turns to the truth or falsity of each of the premises. For each of them, philosophical opinion is divided. So what's wanted then is discussion of each of them, and more argumentation, supporting or defending each. (We'll look at these premises again below.)

THE PARADOX OF JUSTIFICATION

Premises justify a conclusion only if each of them is justified; so it appears we need good arguments to justify each of the premises. But these arguments themselves have premises which need justification. And so on. If everything you assert needs justification, then this appears to be an endless process—an infinite regress, with nowhere to start; and nothing could be justified.

Obviously there's a mistake in here, and it seems pretty clearly to be the idea that everything that's asserted needs justification. Some things can just be asserted—need no justification. So are we back to the idea that we're allowed to say whatever we like?

Not exactly. Practically speaking, when we create arguments, we're allowed to present some premises without justification, ones that can be taken for granted. What sorts of premises are those? Why are we permitted to take them for granted?

MAYBE NEEDS NO JUSTIFICATION: THE SELF-EVIDENT

Some philosophers thought that there were some premises that, by their very nature, didn't need justification. The great philosopher Benedict de Spinoza supported the arguments in his book *Ethics* (1677) with *axioms*—statements that were supposed to be so obviously true that they didn't need any support—and from which he could (he thought) derive everything else he wanted to say. The problems with this are that some of the axioms he provides are rather obscure in meaning (e.g., "Everything which exists, exists either in itself or in something else") or not obviously true (e.g., "The knowledge of an effect depends on and involves the knowledge of a cause") and that not very much can be validly derived from any them—certainly not all that Spinoza claimed could be. But the deeper problem here is why we're supposed to be allowed to take any propositions as axioms, and thus be absolved of the necessity of justifying them.

René Descartes tried the same thing in his *Meditations* (1641), but in his case there was just one starting point—that he is thinking—and he thought he could prove it with no other assumptions. His reasoning is this: My belief that I'm thinking is doubt-proof, because doubting is a kind of thinking. So if I doubt it, it's true. So my belief that I'm thinking couldn't be wrong. From this he drew its immediate consequence: that he exists, at least as a "thing that thinks."

This famous line of reasoning was summed up by Descartes in Latin: Cogito ergo sum ("I think, therefore I am"). (One finds this sentence sometimes on bumper stickers and fridge magnets, and on picket signs protesting the Charlie Hebdo murders, used as a slogan affirming the pre-eminent value of a thoughtful life. It doesn't mean that.)

What's going on here appears more acceptable than Spinoza's version, but many critics have objected that Descartes isn't starting from zero here—that there are hidden assumptions, including that his reasoning power to make this inference is reliable.

> *From the fact of his own existence, he goes on to try to prove the existence of God; this is supposed to underwrite his trust in his reasoning powers, and the general reliability of his senses. It's doubtful whether he can get all that from his starting point. Even though this doesn't seem to work, overall his reputation as one of the greatest of Western philosophers is deserved.*

Sometimes the sort of obviousness that's sought here is what's called *self-evidence.* The notion of a self-evident truth is a rather strange one. 'Self-evident' is often defined as *containing its own evidence or proof.* How can any statement do this? *X* is evidence for *Y* when the truth of *X* makes it more probable (or definite) that *Y* is true. But can a statement be evidence (or proof) for itself? That must be when ... um ... its truth makes it more probable (or definite) that it's true? No, evidence for *Y* has to be something other than *Y*. But we're probably taking the term 'self-evident' a little too narrowly. What's meant is more likely that a self-evident truth is a truth that needs no evidence, because all you have to do to see that it's true is to understand it. Well, okay, but we still need to know how that's supposed to work.

 A famous claim for self-evidence is in the US *Declaration of Independence: "We hold these truths to be self-evident, that all men are created equal, that they are endowed by their Creator with certain unalienable rights [i.e., rights that are not transferable or capable of being repudiated], that among these are life, liberty and the pursuit of happiness." You may well agree that we should be equal and have basic rights, but you don't have to look far to find smart people who disagree; so these claims are hardly self-evident.*

MAYBE NEEDS NO JUSTIFICATION: COMMON SENSE

One of the problems that philosophers are sometimes supposed to spend a lot of time thinking about is whether a world external to our minds exists.

Comic writer Dave Barry's description of philosophy courses in university: "Basically, this involves sitting in a room and deciding there is no such thing as reality and then going to lunch."[31] One of the best cartoons by B. Kliban shows a professor pointing to a blackboard filled with equations and fish symbols, in front of a classroom of attentive fish. The caption is "Proving the existence of fish."[32]

What makes some philosophical proofs seem so silly to people is that what they are trying to establish is *just common sense*—known in a way apparently lacking in philosophers. So maybe here we have a variety of belief that doesn't itself need support by argument, but can be used, unjustified, as a starting point for other arguments.

What's a common-sense belief? It's one we'd all assent to, if asked, though we hardly ever think or talk about it, because it's so obvious. It's one we would find very difficult or impossible to give up.

No doubt there are beliefs like this: that you have a body consisting of various parts (hands, feet, etc.), that there are real people and physical objects outside you (not just hallucinations or dreams), that your senses provide generally good information, and so on. It's sometimes argued that because we are unable to resist these beliefs, the famous (or infamous) philosophical scepticism about these matters cannot get off the ground.

 An influential version of this argument is due to the English philosopher G.E. Moore.[33] When Moore gave a guest lecture at the University of Michigan, he gave an example of something that couldn't possibly be doubted: the existence of that skylight there (he pointed at it) in the ceiling of the auditorium. The audience shifted nervously in their seats, knowing that the skylight was an illusion, backlit to simulate daylight coming through.

On the one hand, common sense appears to provide a suitable sort of starting-point premises—those without need of justification. It does this because a genuine common-sense proposition will already be believed by everyone—they can't help it; and the point of argument is to convince someone of a conclusion by relying on premises that that person will accept.

However, I'd bet you have been in arguments like this:

Al: Why in the world do you think that's true?
Sal: Well, it's only common sense, isn't it?
Al: No it isn't.

Because the real aim of argument is truth, not convincingness, we might wonder why common-sense beliefs are allowable starting points. History shows that various beliefs which everyone has taken to be undeniable common sense have turned out to be false.

> *Chris Daly mentions some pre-scientific common-sense beliefs that have turned out false: that the sun orbits around the earth, that whales are fish, that glass is not a liquid, and that the coldness of an ice cube is transmitted to the drink it floats in. Daly has an enlightening chapter in his book,[34] about the use of common sense in philosophy, and its problems.*

Why think that something that's clearly a matter of common sense is therefore any more likely to be true? Where's the connection between commonsensicality and truth? Why then are common-sense propositions acceptable as premises without themselves having support?

These are questions worthy of serious philosophical consideration; but nevertheless, you should go right ahead and use what seem to you to be perfectly obvious common-sense premises when you need them for argument, without worrying about justifying them. Chances are that others will be willing to accept them without justification also. Anyway, good philosophical writing often lays out its assumptions and shows what follows from them, without assuming that those assumptions are infallible and not open to objection. Even if your readers question these assumptions, they may be interested in seeing, with your help, where they lead.

MAYBE NEEDS NO JUSTIFICATION: EVIDENCE OF YOUR SENSES

Another place where, practically speaking, the receding chain of justification can come to a halt is with the evidence of your own senses. This works best when it comes to beliefs about particular individual objects or events. Your justification for thinking that it's raining outside where you are, at the moment, is that you can see the rain falling outside your window.

While this sort of premise might figure in ordinary day-to-day discussions (e.g., about whether we should drive or walk to the movies), it's questionable whether a particular assertion of this sort can figure as a premise in any philosophical argument. (A venerable tradition, dating back to the ancients, sees knowledge of this sort, about things in the mundane physical world, things that are here today and gone tomorrow, as insignificant, without philosophical consequence, not real knowledge. But you need not accept this judgement.)

And, again, there's a long tradition of philosophical scepticism questioning our sense experience as justification. Our senses do, sometimes, after all, tell us what's false—maybe that's just spray from a lawn sprinkler you see outside—and we get believable but false information when dreaming or hallucinating, or seeing an optical illusion.

CHAPTER 8

WHERE YOU GET TRUE PREMISES: AUTHORITIES

MAYBE NEEDS NO JUSTIFICATION: WHAT AUTHORITIES SAY

Just about every scientific article contains arguments, and the premises for these arguments often contain (non-obvious) premises that are justified by citation of authorities who are thought to have established their truth. It's likely that your arguments for a philosophical position will also be based partly on some non-philosophical non-obvious facts—for example, about the brain, in philosophy of mind; about real languages, in philosophy of language; about consequences of social practices, in political philosophy. Your assertions about these matters also need support in the form of citation of authorities.

The main problem here is whether a source for information is a good enough authority. In some cases, it's perfectly clear that some types of information source are never good enough. When somebody tells you something, that's nowhere good enough, unless that person has appropriate credentials to be an expert on that topic (except on philosophical matters, where there are no experts to vouch for truths). Never trust those bits that get forwarded from one email to another; they're almost invariably false. (Also, I'd recommend that you distrust offers of $180 million from Nigeria.)

A growing source for information nowadays, you don't have to be told, is the Internet, but two facts about web pages mean you should be very careful: (1) they are often produced by a commercial enterprise, eager to sell you something, so the information they give you can be very biased or unfounded or just lies; (2) any energetic crackpot can get web publication for any views whatever. A consequence of these two facts is that what you read on a random website can't be given much trust. Googling turns up a great deal of value, and a bigger deal of cybercrap. (But the Internet is an excellent source for kitten videos.) (Is what I'm saying here the rant of a cranky old guy? Yes! I am a cranky old guy. But it's true that the Internet has plenty of garbage on it.)

You have to know where to look for reliable sources on the Internet, and how to recognize them. Here are some general hints:[35]

- Lots of spelling and grammar errors in what you read in a web page are a good indicator of unreliability. So is a general atmosphere of hysteria. Academic status of the author is some evidence of the trustworthiness of an online article, and of the sanity of its author, but just *some* evidence. Lots of academics publish outlines and summaries on the Internet for their students, and they're often publicly available and pretty good. Some blogs are pretty good, but many are absolutely useless. You can use them for getting ideas, but those ideas need verification.
- Online academic journals are pretty good, usually a much better bet for reliability than random websites. Statistical data should be acquired via academic sources, governmental databases, and reputable polling agencies, not from somebody just mouthing off (who may be just making it up).
- University libraries, by the way, often have highly informed staff eager to help you find reliable information online or in print. Ask.
- *Wikipedia* is often good for a start, but it is to be used with caution. It gets some things completely wrong. Sometimes their cited sources are useful to look at for the whole story.
- The source of lots of "information" in websites is other websites. Misinformation gets passed through virtual space at the speed of light. As with *Wiki*, try to find original sources.

- An unbeatably reliable source for information about philosophical positions is the online *Stanford Encyclopedia of Philosophy* (at Plato.Stanford.edu). Thank you, Stanford!
- There often are well-known and reliable websites for particular fields. For medical facts, for example, you should go to the Johns Hopkins Medicine Health Library or MedlinePlus.gov. Academics in the field you're interested in can tell you about where you should look.
- Excerpts from books, scholarly journals, magazines, and newspapers originally printed on actual *paper* are often available on the Internet.

Paper is very thin, flat, generally white, floppy material, with black marks on it. This was used, in the twentieth century and earlier, for transmitting information. It didn't need electricity! Just imagine.

- Some libraries still have these paper things, and you can go read them there. Book publication doesn't guarantee the authority of the writer, but information in a standard well-known text in the area, published by a company you've heard of, is usually sufficient. Some newspapers are reliable original sources for information, but only a few. At the top of most people's lists for English-language newspapers are *The Guardian* in the UK, and, in the US, *The New York Times*, the *Los Angeles Times*, *The Washington Post*, *The Boston Globe*, and the *Wall Street Journal*. But not the "opinion pieces" in these (or any) newspapers.

AUTHORITY AND TRUTH

When you've found a good authority for a non-obvious non-philosophical assertion, that's conclusive. But note that 'conclusive' just means sufficiently acceptable to require no further justification—it doesn't mean that it's 100 per cent guaranteed true. The history of science shows that sometimes accepted authorities have been wrong. Sometimes the research data behind a claim is just faked, as

with the now infamous article in a very distinguished and author-
itative medical journal claiming that there's a causal link between
vaccination and autism.[36] More often it's an honest mistake. In
1983, Carl Sagan, who was widely respected as a scientist (despite
being a media star), claimed that a series of nuclear explosions
would produce a "nuclear winter"—a global drop in temperature
sufficient for wide-scale extinctions. His (co-authored) article was
published in another highly respected journal.[37] His ideas became
something like scientific orthodoxy, and had wide acceptance
among the general public. But Sagan and his co-authors admitted
in a 1990 article in the same journal that what they wrote was completely wrong.[38]

We can't expect the latest information from mainstream science
to be *perfectly* correct, but why demand perfection? Isn't *very reliable* good enough? What this might mean is that it's possible that
an argument depending on scientific information could be no good.
But, except when the information comes from unreliable or heavily
speculative sources, we can consider the information very probably true. In this sublunary sphere, this is the most we ordinarily can
hope for, and it's ordinarily good enough.

 *In Aristotle's physics, the earth was in the middle of concentric
invisible spheres; the closest of these anchored the moon,
the next the sun, then several for the planets, then the stars.
In the spheres of the moon and up, everything was perfect,
permanent, and necessary; but in the sublunary (below
the moon) sphere containing the earth, things were flawed,
temporary, contingent, and variable.*

Okay, but since we're philosophers, we should consider a bizarre
sceptical question (which should not, for practical purposes, be
taken seriously): Why does science have any degree of trustworthiness at all? Science done well is science that meets its own method-
ological criteria, but why think that this has anything at all to do with
truth—which is, after all, what we're after? From one perspective,
science appears to be a game with its own arbitrary rules, and its
own respected experts who get to give each other the warrant to

make assertions when the rules are followed. Could the whole thing be completely detached from reality? (More about this later.)

CITING PHILOSOPHERS

We've been talking about truth and justification of assertions about non-philosophical matters; let's now consider philosophical assertions.

There's a sharp difference in philosophy from many other fields. Writing in many other fields contains a large amount of citation of authorities, when it's thought that matters are settled, or at least strongly enough confirmed. But philosophy, as we have seen, is unusual in that everything is an open question. So you can't just cite the writings of an earlier philosopher, and consider the matter settled. You can't get away with saying, "As Aristotle [or Spinoza or Berkeley or Wittgenstein] showed...."

Aquinas, whom we referred to above as a paradigm of taking counter-argument seriously, also, however, was quite happy to claim the backing of authorities, including the Bible, St. Augustine, other official church theologians, and especially Aristotle. But in every case he does give his own arguments, so it's not really clear how seriously we should take this. What any of these authorities really meant is often (especially in the case of Aristotle) difficult to interpret, and Aquinas sometimes appears to interpret them in ways suspiciously suitable for his own positions. Maybe these appeals to authority are just window dressing. Aquinas himself became the authority for future Catholic theology and philosophy, sometimes to the detriment of genuine argument.

Of course, you can refer to the positions of earlier philosophers, in order to discuss those positions and maybe argue for or against them, but you can't assume that they settled anything, that they are accepted authorities for the truth of any of their positions. (Again you should note that some philosophers do try to get away with this, relying on their favourite doctrine or author instead of on real argument. Beware of this sort of philosopher.)

But you can and should cite another philosopher from whom you got an idea. This is not using that philosopher as an authority on the subject—not providing any grounds for thinking the idea is true—but rather giving credit for the idea.

CITING OTHER WORKS

Here's something very important: WHENEVER WHAT YOU WRITE HAS ITS SOURCE IN SOMEBODY ELSE'S WORDS OR IDEAS, YOU MUST CITE THAT SOURCE in a footnote or in parentheses in the text. At the end of this book, you'll find an appendix with information about the form these citations should have.

There are several good reasons why you should include these citations. For one thing, it is often helpful to refer readers to the books or articles that are the sources for your ideas, so they can look at those sources to see if you got them right. But also, so they can find what more to read about the issues under discussion—and thus citations are like "For Further Reading" sections.

But citations are not just helps for the reader. They are morally—even to some extent legally—required. If what you're writing is a class assignment, the default assumption is that the words and ideas in what you hand in will be yours, not somebody else's. So when what you write isn't entirely yours, you need to note that fact. The rule is: the source of every idea not your own must be footnoted. Not just direct quotes from other writings, but even your own paraphrases. This is news to some beginning writers. I found a long paper I wrote in maybe grade nine, and it contains, without footnotes, long passages obviously written in encyclopedese, clearly copied verbatim. In high school you can sometimes get away with this, but by the time you get serious, in university or afterwards, this rule is taken seriously.

Without that citation, you're taking credit for what you haven't created—that's theft. It's called plagiarism, and is sometimes severely punished by your teacher or by a school committee set up to adjudicate and impose sanctions in these matters. If what you're writing is just a small assignment, and you've just failed to write a footnote for an idea or phrase or sentence you got from a book, then that's not the end of the world, and will probably just result in a suggestion written on your paper by the grader. But failing to credit larger portions of what you write is more serious. Even worse, and very serious indeed, is copying larger passages from somewhere, or submitting a purchased pre-written paper. The Internet has made this sort of academic crime much easier. You can find a paper-mill which will sell you a paper, or write one for you, and maybe the result will not be very terrible; or you can easily cut-and-paste from a philosophy Internet site. But the ease of doing this has made it more common; as a result, graders are much more sensitive to signs of it in your writing, and are very good at detecting it. There are even fairly effective apps for them to use to check on possible plagiarism. There are often very serious consequences. Don't do it!

Plagiarism outside of class—in a book or article you publish—can result in legal trouble. This can be even worse than academic trouble.

But sometimes it's not exactly clear whether or not you need to footnote an idea. A long time ago, I was trying to write my thesis, and the writing was stalled till I came up with an idea about solving the problem I chose to write on. After that the writing came easily. But just before I got to show all my magnificent work to my thesis adviser, I discovered that a very famous twentieth-century philosopher had solved that very problem with that very idea, and had written it all up in a book I should have read. A PhD thesis is supposed to be original research. I went to my thesis adviser and, crestfallen, told him about this. He said, "Don't worry! Every idea has been expressed by some philosopher in writing somewhere. You can still use this idea. Just stick in a footnote saying, "Professor Blahblah has suggested a position somewhat like this in his book, *Treatise on SuchandSuch*."

My adviser was right. Every idea you can think of has already been thought of, and written about, by some other philosopher. So is there no such thing as original philosophy? Is all legitimate philosophical writing just reporting what someone else has said? Well, not exactly. When what you're writing is a major paper (a thesis, for example) you should do what I didn't: survey the *major* literature in the area, and footnote your idea mentioning previous writing which it resembles. For a smaller paper (for example, one of several assignments in a class) you might look at a few other published sources, or maybe just bounce your ideas off a single assigned reading. You should footnote these sources, but you needn't do any large-scale literature survey.

This, by the way, is a good method for writing a philosophy paper. Read an assigned bit of philosophy you think is mistaken, and then write down why you think it's wrong, and (maybe) defend what you think is correct. It's easy to find something you think is wrong. (This, by the way, is what made me consider going into philosophy. When I was a kid, I blundered into a book of Plato's dialogues. Everywhere I read in it, I thought I detected mistaken positions and bad reasoning. The cover of the book announced "Plato is philosophy, and philosophy Plato!" so I thought that if I knew better than the world's champion philosopher, that was the game for me.)

It's usually expected that what you write in philosophy represents some degree of thought on your own. So it's not acceptable merely to find something that somebody has written and paraphrase it. You'll have to add some angle or twist of your own, even if it is a small one. Sorry to have to tell you this: the ideas you've thought of have occurred somewhere in the philosophical literature where they are explained and defended better than you could do. Don't let this bother you. Be reasonable. You should give citations for the sources you use, but you don't need to cite the 5,134,662 websites or the 7,420 books that Google will turn up for your idea.

CHAPTER 9

WHERE YOU GET TRUE PREMISES: ANALYSIS

Consider this version of an argument we looked at a while back:

- Premise (1): Human beings are sometimes responsible for their actions.
- Premise (2): You're responsible for an action only if you could have done otherwise.
- Premise (3): You could have done otherwise only if pre-existent causes did not determine your action.

What—if anything—allows a philosopher to make these claims? Let's just concentrate on premise (2) (although the other two are controversial).

Is premise (2) just obvious? Some philosophers would say that it's a conceptual truth—something you'd be expected to believe because it's *part of the concept* of responsibility that to be responsible one must have been able to do otherwise. You're supposed to be able to find that out for yourself, just by reflecting on the concept of responsibility. If you don't see immediately that it involves being able to act otherwise, some examples might help. Consider a story about somebody who did something bad but who couldn't have done otherwise: baby Clarissa has fallen into the deep end of a swimming pool, but Fred doesn't jump in and swim over to save her. Why not? Because Fred can't swim. He *couldn't* have swum over to save her. He did look around for a long pole to push out to her—there wasn't any— and he did yell for help, but there was nobody else around. It's awful that baby Clarissa has drowned, and we sympathize with Fred who wanted to do something but couldn't, but we don't hold him morally responsible for not saving Clarissa. Under the circumstances, he couldn't have done otherwise.

Now compare the case of Sally, who, when little Sylvester fell into that swimming pool, chose not to jump in and save him because she didn't like little Sylvester and anyway she didn't feel like getting her hair wet. She could have jumped in and saved him, but she didn't. She is morally responsible for what she did (and didn't do).

Thinking about moral responsibility, perhaps with nudges from examples like this, shows that the ability to do otherwise is built into the concept of moral responsibility (or the term 'moral responsibility'), as a necessary application condition. Somebody who blamed Fred—who thought he was morally to blame in Clarissa's drowning—just doesn't understand the words 'moral responsibility' (or the concept they stand for).

The philosophical activity of drawing out what's involved in a term like 'moral responsibility' (for use, as above, in an argument) is called *philosophical analysis*.

 Is what gets analysed terms (words or phrases) or the concepts (or properties) they refer to? This is a question that we're not going to get into. I'll just ignore that subtlety here, and skip back and forth in a messy way, instead of mentioning both possibilities every time.

Philosophical analysis, at times and among some philosophers, was counted as a central task of philosophy— maybe even the *central task. The importance of analysis to the work of a group of twentieth-century mostly English-speaking philosophers resulted in their being called "analytic philosophers" (a name that has more or less fallen into disuse).*

Well, what's going on in a philosophical analysis? Is it merely defining a word (or phrase)? Not exactly. Here's what you get when you look up the definition of 'moral responsibility': "The status of morally deserving praise, blame, reward, or punishment for an act or omission, in accordance with one's moral obligations."[39] But that doesn't tell us what moral responsibility *really is*. It doesn't tell us what moral responsibility involves, how to tell whether it applies in some difficult cases, what the basis for application is, or what's supposed to be the reason why in some cases praise or reward/blame or punishment are appropriate reactions to good/bad actions, but in other cases they aren't. Sometimes what's really going on in analysis is far more than merely finding a synonym for words; it's rather taking a complicated concept and breaking it down into its component concepts, thus revealing its essential application conditions, and demonstrating its connections with other concepts.

Well, all of that is quite abstract, and maybe you don't exactly get the idea. I think what might help is to look at some examples.

Consider this question: What is knowledge? The online Merriam-Webster dictionary app for my word processor is remarkably unhelpful in defining 'knowledge': "the fact or condition of knowing something with familiarity gained through experience or association." Well, okay, so we're referred to 'knowing', which is defined as "acquaintance, cognizance." So let's try 'cognizance'. That's defined as "knowledge, awareness." This is not going anywhere. Yes, that online dictionary gives only very minimal definitions. *The American Heritage Dictionary of the English Language* has more. Their definition as "the state or fact of knowing" sends us to the verb 'know': "1. To perceive directly with the senses or mind; apprehend with clarity or certainty.... 2. To be certain of; regard or accept as true beyond doubt...." That's not much help either. So if Fred regards the (false) proposition that the Franco-Prussian War began in 1880 as true beyond doubt, then he knows it? No, that doesn't seem right. And if Sally was very confident that it began in 1870, and she's right, but that's just a very lucky guess, is that knowledge? The problem with definitions is not just that they (sometimes) seem to get things wrong, but that they're uninformative: they really don't tell us how to apply the term.

What we need instead is an analysis: *X is knowledge if and only if....* In other words: we need to be provided with a set of conditions which are individually necessary and jointly sufficient for application of that term. How about this:

S knows that *p* if and only if :
(a) *S* believes that *p*

(b) p is true

(c) S has good reason to believe p (that is, S is justified in believing p).

Well, that's progress. Turns out that this analysis isn't exactly right (see below), but anyway it's the kind of thing that we're looking for. It attempts to give application conditions for the terms.

Okay, here come some more examples of analyses that have been proposed for philosophically important terms. (What the correct analysis is, in each case, is controversial. Some of the attempts at analysis below are obviously incorrect.)

- What is justice? Proposed analysis: Justice is the power of securing good things.[40]
- What is a morally permissible act? Proposed analysis: A morally permissible act is one that doesn't treat anybody merely as a means to an end.[41]
- What is the morally best act? Proposed analysis: It's the act, among the possible alternatives, that results in the greatest net gain in happiness among all those affected.[42]
- What is it to be a person? Proposed analysis: A person is an organism which is capable of self-awareness.
- What are mental-state ascriptions (e.g., "Fred is sad")? Proposed analysis: They are claims about how people are behaving, or are disposed to behave. (This analysis, no longer given much credence, was provided by analytic behaviourism.)

JUSTIFYING AND REFUTING ANALYSES

An analysis you accept can be used as a premise in an argument. If you're doing medical ethics, for example, you might use that analysis of 'morally permissible' as part of the argument against the moral acceptability of a certain medical practice which you claim, in another premise, treats people—some people—as mere means. Of course, these analysis premises (and your other premises) may themselves be controversial and need support. And may of course be subject to counter-argument from others.

How do you test—confirm or refute—an analysis claim? It's hard to think about them just in the abstract: do you get any answer when you consider those examples above and ask yourself whether, in each case, that's what your concept involves? A much better way is to consider hypothetical cases.

The premise about responsibility, considered above, is to some degree confirmed by cases that agree with it. When you read about the Fred/Sally hypothetical cases (about Clarissa's drowning), was your reaction that Sally is responsible, but Fred is not? If so, that makes the analysis under consideration a bit more plausible. But a hypothetical case in which somebody could not have done otherwise, but is nevertheless responsible for what he/she did (or did not do) would refute it. It's a *counter-example* to this analysis. Here, perhaps, is one such case: Porky is inside the house with that swimming pool in the backyard. He idly glances out the window, and sees little Sam falling in. (No surprise to us: babies fall in here regularly. Why don't they put a fence up?) "Well, it's not my problem," says Porky to himself, and resumes downloading Internet porn (the swine!). But here's the tricky part: unknown to Porky, the only door leading to the back yard is locked from the outside, and Porky wouldn't be able to get out if he tried. So he could not have saved little Sam. So, according to the proposed analysis, Porky is not morally responsible in Sam's death, and we should just say, "Well, too bad, Porky, you couldn't have saved Sam anyway." That's right—he couldn't have—but it's clearly absurd to absolve him. We all, it seems, have the intuition that Porky is to blame in this case, even though he in fact couldn't have done otherwise. In that case, the proposed analysis is wrong.

Consider another attempted analysis on our list: *knowledge* is justified true belief. Some hypothetical examples add plausibility to this analysis.

- Suppose Merv looks at you blankly when you ask him if it's snowing in Lhasa (the capital of Tibet). He hadn't ever thought about Lhasa, or the weather there, till you asked him, and he has no beliefs about it at all. So (according to this analysis) he doesn't know that it's snowing in Lhasa.

- Or suppose Merv believes that it's snowing in Lhasa but it isn't, then (according to this analysis) he doesn't know that it's snowing in Lhasa.
- Or suppose Merv believes that it's snowing in Lhasa, and it is; but he's just made a lucky guess, so his true belief isn't justified. Then (according to this analysis) he doesn't know that it's snowing in Lhasa.
- Or suppose Merv believes that it's snowing in Lhasa, and he's right. He believes this because he's just checked out AccuWeather.com for Lhasa, which predicted lots of continuous snow all day there. This is a source of reliable short-term weather reports, so he's justified in his belief. Then (according to this analysis) he does know it's snowing in Lhasa.

All these applications of the analysis seem to come out right. That is to say: you're a competent user of the concept *knowledge*, and when you consider these hypothetical situations and apply that concept, to see whether Merv knows that it's snowing in Lhasa or not in each case, you come out (let's assume) with the same answer that is given by this proposed analysis. So far that analysis looks pretty good.

However all that it takes for rejection of a proposed analysis is a convincing *counter-example*. These are hypothetical cases that come in two sorts: those in which the analysis tells us we have an instance of that concept, but we don't; and those in which the analysis tells us that we don't have an instance of that concept, but we do. So the *knowledge* analysis might be refuted by a hypothetical case of justified true belief that isn't knowledge, or by a case of knowledge that isn't justified true belief.

Here we propose one of each, with guesses at what YOUR REACTION might be:

- Suppose that one afternoon Lucy looks at her watch, which says 2:30. Her watch is very reliable: she's had it for years, and it's never been off more than a minute or two, so she believes that it's just about 2:30. She's justified, because her watch has a long history of reliability. Her belief is true, because in fact it is 2:30. But the trick is that the battery in her watch ran out, by coincidence, at 2:30 the previous morning.

YOUR REACTION: This means that Sally doesn't know that it's 2:30, even though her belief that it's 2:30 is true and justified. (Are you worried about the assertion that she's justified, given that her watch is broken? Well, a justified belief [and here comes another analysis] is one supported by very good [but not necessarily infallible] evidence. Sally has this sort of belief. Ok, so maybe you're worried about the assertion that she has very good evidence? But [a third analysis]: there can be very good evidence for a false proposition.

• Suppose that Mortimer is being quizzed on the history of the British monarchy.

"Who succeeded Henry VI?" he's asked.

He replies, "I don't have a clue."

"Just guess," he's urged.

"Okay, oh well, um, Edward IV."

"Do you really think so?"

"No, of course not! That's just a guess. I just pulled that name out of the blue."

But Mortimer's answer is correct, and he also identifies the following monarchs as Edward V, Richard III, and Henry VII, despite his continuing protests that he has no idea of the answers.

YOUR REACTION: Mortimer's answers are true, and somehow justified (or else he wouldn't have been consistently right). Marvin doesn't believe that Edward IV succeeded Henry VI, but he knows it![43]

A PRIORI

It's often claimed that analytic premises—those based on conceptual analysis—can be known *a priori*. (That's Latin, meaning "from what comes before.") What that means is that they don't require any *empirical investigation*—any evidence of the senses—for their justification. Their truth is just a consequence of the concept involved. Of course, (some philosophers insist) you needed to have sensory contact with the outside world to learn the concepts in the first place, but once you have them, that's all you need to know the truth of the analytic premise. So, for example, in a much simpler case, once you understand the concept of *uncle*, you'd know that someone introduced to you as Abagail's uncle has to be the brother of one of her parents. You wouldn't have to undertake any empirical investigation to determine this. The contrast here is with knowledge *a posteriori* (Latin: "from what comes after")—that needs someone's sense-investigation for justification. The claim that one's uncle is most likely to share 25 per cent of one's genetic make-up is a posteriori—can't be known merely by examination of the concepts involved. Empirical investigation is necessary.

In this case, as in some others, what is knowable a priori is also not terribly important information. Consider these examples from newspapers (quoted in numerous websites, from unidentified issues of The New Yorker *magazine):*

- *Businesses planning sales strategists perceive buying power as a gauge of the general ability of potential customers to buy their products.* (Chicago Sun-Times)
- *The task force said it looked at hunger as a social problem in which some people cannot obtain adequate amounts of food.* (The Boston Globe)
- *"Much too frequently, the criminal escapes the scene of a crime because he manages to escape the visual capability of the responding officers," said Monterey Park Police Chief Jon Elder.* (Los Angeles Times)

On the other hand, a correct analysis is not trivial. And one of the major controversies in philosophy has been whether there is a priori knowledge that is neither trivial nor a matter of analysis. Kant held, for example, that the claim "Every event has a cause" is known a priori, though not trivial or analytic.

This is significant because the a priori is often seen as a distinctive feature of philosophy. Philosophers, after all (according to the traditional view), don't have labs, don't collect data, don't make observations. They just sit around and think (traditionally in armchairs, though philosophy departments nowadays can't afford this essential philosophical tool). I don't mean that their answers just magically suddenly come to them out of the blue. They have to do a lot of reading, research, and discussion. But still, they don't have to do empirical investigation.

This idea has recently been challenged by philosophers who believe that philosophical methods are (or should be) experimental—that is, should use empirical investigation even for conceptual analysis. One way this might make sense is to distribute questionnaires to find out how people actually do apply concepts. The more conventional view is that each of us is familiar with the term or concept, so we don't have to ask anyone else how it's applied.

The odd notion that just sitting around and thinking can produce any conclusions worth knowing is, perhaps, given some sense when we think that this procedure might produce analytic truths—conceptual truths such as the ones we've been looking at—that are useful in philosophical arguments.

Philosophers sometimes say that we consult our "intuitions" when we consider cases like that of Fred and Sally above. We have an intuition that Fred is not morally responsible and that Sally is. Don't confuse this sort of thing with what we ordinarily call by that name: an 'intuition' in our ordinary way of speaking is something that's just immediately known by somebody. They just "get" it, not on the basis of observation or reasoning, but as a sort of instinctive feeling: a guess, but a mysteriously reliable guess. Philosophical intuitions are related to ordinary ones, in that they don't need rational proof, scientific authority, confirmation by empirical observation, or anything like that. When you assent to the proposition that a person is responsible only when that person could have done otherwise, it just clearly appears true to you; but the basis of this belief is no mystery. It arises from your having the concept of responsibility—knowing how to apply it; its correct application is to cases in which the person in question had the ability to do otherwise. It's like the way you know that ducks are animals, not automobiles or peanut butter sandwiches: anyone who thinks otherwise just doesn't have the concept of duck-ness, or hasn't thought about it sufficiently.

QUESTIONS ABOUT ANALYSIS

A problem with some proposed analyses is that it's not altogether clear whether something is involved in a particular concept or not, either because the concepts are vague, with fuzzy boundaries, or because they weren't designed to handle weird cases. Here are some examples which are sort of cute, though not particularly loaded with philosophical significance:

- House-trailer owners sometimes park the things fairly permanently, propping them up on concrete blocks, connecting them to electricity and plumbing and telephone, planting gardens around them, etc. Municipalities always have different zoning and taxation regulations for "vehicles" and for "dwellings." Which one do we have here?[44]
- Foods are classified as meat, fish, starches, fruit, vegetables, etc. Is a cucumber a vegetable? Or is it a fruit (because it's the part of the plant that bears seeds)? If it's a vegetable, then how about pickle relish?

> *During the 1980s, school lunch programmes in the us were having problems because of reduced government subsidy. In response, the us nutrition agency which required a vegetable in subsidized lunches allowed pickle relish to count as a vegetable.*

- Chimpanzees and humans, it's alleged, can interbreed.[45] Would the offspring have human rights?

Shortly, in the section called "The Thought Experiment," we'll look at some examples of philosophical controversies some of which may seem to result from weird and extraordinary examples that ordinary concepts aren't designed to handle.

THE PRACTICALITY OF ARGUMENTATION

We've been looking at, and criticizing, various views on what might count as a premise for an argument that needs no justification. There are possible problems with each of these views, of course; after all, the question concerning where one is allowed to start from in arguing is itself a philosophical question.

Practically speaking, however, the philosophically problematic nature of any sort of starting point should not stop you from starting to argue. What you need to convince others of is not a starting point that can be shown objectively and permanently to need no justifica‑ tion; what you need is a starting point that they will accept. When you're right—when they do grant you your premises—then this is good; if they agree that the logic of your argument is acceptable, then they should, if they're rational, accept your conclusion.

But this ideal situation is sometimes not what goes on in actual philosophical arguments. When you offer a premise as a starting point that you hope your audience will take for granted, but they question it, then you might have to justify it, and that regress con‑ tinues. It seems that, in philosophy anyway, nothing is immune from question; no matter what philosophical premise you offer, you might find a philosopher who refuses to take it for granted, even when the alternative is weird and bizarre. (Remember that quotation from Descartes I mentioned earlier about the strange and unbelievable things some philosophers believe?)

When this is serious, not just frivolous questioning of everything (as your favourite five-year-old does), this is philosophy doing its job the way it should. In philosophy, then, it appears that arguments can go only so far, performing a one or a few justificatory steps; at that point, they invite consideration of the next steps. Nothing is neces‑ sarily final—everything can be part of a process which won't come to a permanent end. That's the pattern shown by the history of philoso‑ phy: continual motion and progress, re-evaluation, reconsideration; and the old questions coming up anew.

But even if your audience will not grant your starting point, they may find your argument worthwhile if you draw interesting consequences from that point. I have been insisting that the primary job of philosophers is to present and convince others of truth. But there is also a good deal of intrinsic interest in looking at ingenious arguments that start from false premises, even though, as we've seen, they will not be good arguments for their conclusions. This is a good deal of the charm you might find in reading, for example, ancient or medieval philosophers. They often start with premises that they take for granted, but that seem to most of us nowadays to be false, even absurdly so. But those philosophers are often very smart, and it can be fascinating seeing what conclusions they draw. This is sort of similar to the attraction of more advanced mathematics: even though it may be totally inapplicable to reality, it can still be amazing.

CHAPTER 10

THE THOUGHT EXPERIMENT

IMAGINARY EXPERIMENTS

A thought experiment is, as it says, an imaginary experiment. Very often, it isn't—sometimes even can't be—carried out in reality. Its purpose is to show unexpected consequences, sometimes contradictions—flowing from what we imagine, or what we already believe. (This is closely related to the hypothetical-example test for proposed analyses, that we just examined.)

Here are several examples of famous thought experiments.

1. Lucretius' Infinite Universe

The brilliant ancient Roman philosopher/poet Lucretius (first century BCE) came up with this proof that the universe is infinite—that is, without boundaries. Imagine, Lucretius urges us, instead that the universe is finite. That means it has boundaries. Now imagine that you're standing right next to one of the boundaries, and you throw a spear at it. What happens? Either it goes through the boundary, to the other side, in which case that boundary has something on the other side of it. Or it bounces off the boundary; but a boundary is a dividing wall, implying that it walls off this space from that one. In either case, the boundary is not the edge of the universe; so imagining a boundary leads to a contradiction. There is no boundary, so the universe is infinite.[46]

 Almost 2,000 years later Einsteinian physics replaced the idea of a boundless infinite universe with the idea that space

*doesn't have boundaries, but is nevertheless finite. That means
that if you start right here, and travel in a straight line in any
direction, you'll never reach an edge of the universe. (So no
boundaries.) But it's not infinite, because you'll eventually
come back to where you started. (Doesn't that mean that you
weren't travelling in a straight line? No, but I'm not going to try
to explain that any further.)*

*Lucretius also dismissed the idea that the world is a sphere,
because he found the idea of people and animals on the other
side walking around upside-down ridiculous.*[47] *Oh well.*

2. Galileo's Falling Bodies

Until Galileo (1564–1642) claimed otherwise, people believed what
Aristotle had taught: that heavier bodies fall faster than light ones.
Well, they often do: bowling balls do fall faster than feathers, because
air resistance is more significant on low-density spread-out objects;
but discounting that, contrary to Aristotle, they would fall equally
fast. Here's Galileo's disproof. Imagine you're on the Leaning Tower
of Pisa, and you have two objects with different weights—for example, a heavy cannonball and a light musket ball. If Aristotle were right
and you dropped both off the tower simultaneously, the cannonball would hit the ground first. Now imagine that you tied the two
objects together with a chain, and dropped that composite object off.
If Aristotle were right, the cannonball would try to go faster, pulling the slower musket ball along, and the chain would go taut. The
pair would go slower than the cannonball falling alone, and faster
than the musket ball alone. But on the other hand, the two objects
chained together constitute a new object heavier than either ball by
itself. So if Aristotle were right, the pair would fall faster than either
ball falling by itself. Aristotle's view results in a contradiction. It has
to be wrong.

3. The Laws of Shadows

Here are the two Laws of Shadows everyone believes: (1) Something
not illuminated does not cast a shadow. (2) The shadow of something
illuminated is cast on, and "stopped by," the first opaque object it
encounters, without "going through" it.

Now imagine this experiment: you have a light source, a screen, a bowling ball, and a coffee mug. A light behind the coffee mug would cast a shadow on the screen.

Now let's add the bowling ball between the light source and the coffee mug. It totally shades the coffee mug, and casts a bigger shadow on the screen.

Now consider the coffee-mug-shaped portion of the shadow of the bowling ball on the line between the light source and the coffee mug extended to the screen. I've coloured this portion grey, but it's really black shadow.

What is casting this part of the shadow? It cannot be the coffee cup, because that's not illuminated, and, as rule (1) says, something that's not illuminated does not cast a shadow. It cannot be the bowling ball, because the opaque coffee cup comes between the bowling ball and that section of shadow, and, as rule (2) says, shadows do not pass through opaque objects.

So we have proven, by mere thought experiment, that those laws of shadows cannot both be true.[48]

4. Time Travel Paradox

You're all familiar with this one from many movies. Imagine that there's a time machine that could send you back into the past, and that what you wanted to do there was to kill your own evil grandfather when he was still an infant, so that he wouldn't later do all those horrible things he eventually did to your family. But then he would never have married your grandmother, so your father would never have been born, and neither would you. In that case, who killed him? That's impossible.

> *This idea has received so much philosophical attention that it has merited a standard name: the grandfather paradox. Among its very interesting treatments, I recommend a 1976 article by David Lewis.*[49] *He argues that it's not impossible that you kill your grandfather. It's just that you happen not to have done it (maybe your gun jams, or something). After all, grampa survived, right?*

These four thought experiments are a priori arguments against factual hypotheses. That's very peculiar—we'd normally expect arguments against (or for) factual hypotheses to be the exclusive domain of empirical science. In these examples, however, hypotheses are criticized by drawing out their apparently contradictory consequences. But now, instead, let's look at some thought experiments that attempt to justify or refute philosophical positions.

PHILOSOPHICAL THOUGHT EXPERIMENTS

First, three ethics thought experiments.

1. The Parasite Violinist

This thought experiment aims at convincing people that abortion is ethically permitted. Imagine you wake up one morning with a famous violinist in bed with you. "What's going on here?" you yell. People explain to you that the violinist has a fatal disease, and would die unless attached to someone else's blood supply for nine months. Because you have the necessary rare blood type, she was attached to you while you're asleep, so in order to keep her alive, you're going to have to bear with it. The attached violinist will be a major problem to you in your everyday life for that time, but detaching her would mean her death. The intuition you're encouraged to have here is that, even though you'd be an enormously good Samaritan to keep the violinist alive, worthy of praise from music lovers everywhere, you're permitted to detach her. Whatever her "right to life" involves, it does not entitle her to use your body, with substantial cost to you, to stay alive.[50]

The analogy, of course, is supposed to extend to a fetus dependent on a woman's body for its life. Even if a fetus is developed enough to merit full human rights (which has of course been debated), its right to life does not mean that it is entitled to use its mother, at substantial cost to mom, to keep it alive.

There are two main issues here. First of all, are your intuitions that you're permitted to end the violinist's life? If so, then the rule that ending an innocent person's life is always ethically impermissible is mistaken. And second: even if you agree that it's permitted under some circumstances, is a mother carrying a fetus one of them? After all, it's pointed out, fetuses often arrive by conscious invitation by the mother, who is aware of the responsibility for the fetus's life she is taking on. But what about unintentional pregnancies, and those resulting from rape? (Studies show that approximately half of pregnancies in the US are unintentional, and that half of these end in abortion.[51])

2. The Spelunkers

This thought experiment is designed to reveal intuitions favourable to utilitarianism. That's the view that the morally best action is the one that results in the greatest sum total of benefit for everyone. (That might sound pretty obvious, but just wait.)

A group of 10 people are exploring a seaside cave. Suddenly a huge rock falls filling up most of the cave entrance. They let Jaiden, who is the largest person in the group, try to get out first through the small opening remaining, but he gets stuck halfway out. The rest of the group, who are smaller than Jaiden, could get through the opening if Jaiden weren't stuck in it. The tide is coming in and they'll all drown except for Jaiden (whose head is sticking out of the cave) if nothing is done. One person in the group has a stick of dynamite— not enough to blast away the rock, but enough to blast Jaiden out of the opening. Should they do it? Your intuition is supposed to be: nine deaths if they don't blast Jaiden out; one death if they do. So blast him out.[52]

3. The Evil Surgeon

But this thought experiment is produced by anti-utilitarians. Dr. Ella, the transplant surgeon, has nine people in her hospital waiting for various organs that would save their lives; but no organs are available. While worrying about this, she glances out the window, and sees Old Mouldy, a homeless person who spends his days sitting on the bench outside the hospital. She thinks: "I could send a couple of burly hospital orderlies out there to grab Old Mouldy and drag him in to the operating room, where I would anaesthetize him and cut him up to harvest the organs that would save my nine patients. He's healthy, so his organs will be okay. He has no friends or relatives that would mourn his death. Nobody would ever know what became of him, in fact." Should she do it? There will be nine deaths if she does nothing; one death if she cuts up Old Mouldy. Maybe your intuition is that she can't just kill him like that. She just has to let the nine die.[53]

Notice that the intuition I imagine you get thinking about the spelunkers thought experiment supports a general theory (more or less, that the fewer deaths the better) which is the opposite of the one supported by the evil surgeon experiment. What's going on here?

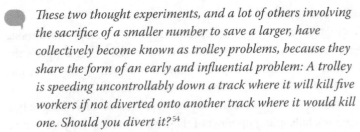

These two thought experiments, and a lot of others involving the sacrifice of a smaller number to save a larger, have collectively become known as trolley problems, because they share the form of an early and influential problem: A trolley is speeding uncontrollably down a track where it will kill five workers if not diverted onto another track where it would kill one. Should you divert it?[54]

An earlier version of the spelunker problem—maybe the earliest, and certainly the most disgusting—imagines that everyone's trapped in the cave, and will all starve before rescue can get to them. Should they kill and eat one of their number?[55]

Maybe the cave and surgeon cases are not parallel. Surgeons, after all, have responsibilities because of their special role, and the greater good in the long run might not result from their killing a random person. Might this be what pushed you to the intuition that Dr. Ella shouldn't do it? (If you had that intuition!)

These thought experiments (like many others in philosophy) rely on our intuitions about bizarre cases, and it's possible that there are no reliable intuitions about these cases. Any reactions we might have in cases like these, it has been argued, are just idle fantasy. This is because our concepts, perfectly serviceable in the real world of ordinary cases, are just not set up to deal with weird cases like this—they don't give us any determinate answer.

Some philosophers have criticized thought experiments like these because, they claim, the imaginary stories told are "intuition pumps"[56]—stories designed to manipulate our intuitions to prove a point. If the intuition is created by the story, then it fails to be the evidence that the story is designed to support. Intuitions are intended to reveal what a concept involves. But pumped intuitions don't do this. They distort an existing concept, or create a new different one.

Some feminist philosophers are especially wary of thought experiments aiming at ethical conclusions, for a slightly different reason. It's not just that these cases are bizarre; it's that they're so oversimplified. Reliable ethical intuitions are those that react to real-life cases that are inevitably complex—where there's a very long story to be told, full of particular details. What we should do to develop and hone our ethical reactions, they urge, is concentrate instead on real, or at least realistic, individual, concrete cases, in all their complex detail. Who exactly are those people in the cave? How did they get there? What are they like? What about their families, and their jobs, and their other relationships? This sort of thinking might reveal genuine moral reactions. Hugely oversimplified 10-to-1 cases reveal nothing. Ethics is not a matter of the application of simplistic principles. It's a matter of attending to particular cases, in all their great detail.[57]

Now for some thought experiments not about ethics.

4. Zombies

"Materialism," in ordinary talk, is an attitude that emphasizes material possessions over intellectual or spiritual matters. But as a technical term in philosophy, it names the position that physical matter is what everything is made of, and that everything (including humans) is explainable by physical processes and laws. So philosophical materialists believe that humans are nothing but extremely complicated physical mechanisms, and that our conscious experiences are nothing but certain kinds of physical interactions in our bodies. In other words, they hold that that there is no separate entity called the mind; the mind just is the body (well, the brain in particular). So each mental event just is a brain event.

But the contemporary philosopher David Chalmers deploys a thought experiment against that belief, as follows.[58] Imagine a world including zombies. We're not talking about the flesh-eating undead monsters that stagger so enjoyably around third-rate movies. The zombies philosophers talk about look and act just like us, with physical bodies exactly like ours inside and out. The only difference between them and us is that they have no mental life—no internal experience. They act angry, but don't feel angry. They can pick out the red marbles from a bowl of marbles of all colours, but they don't have the experience we have of seeing something red. There's nothing that it's like to be one of them. Got the picture? Well, if this possibility makes sense to you, then that shows that it's possible to have exactly our physical make-up without our conscious events. But if mental events were brain events, then this would be necessary, the same way that, since water is H_2O, then it's necessary that each sample of water is H_2O. (If something weren't H_2O, then it couldn't be water.)

There's a lot that needs explanation in here, and some of the assumptions behind this argument are controversial. One might question, for example, that the idea of zombies we think we have doesn't show that they're (in some sense) possible. Or the idea that if X just is Y, then that's a necessary fact—couldn't be otherwise. And again, maybe you don't share the intuition that zombies are possible, or don't have any intuitions about the matter, or are having your intuitions "pumped." But this is not the place to go further into this interesting and complicated subject.

5. Twin-Earth

Imagine that there's a planet in another solar system exactly like ours—an atom-by-atom duplicate of Earth and just about everything on it; call that planet Twin-Earth. (Never mind how improbable the existence of Twin-Earth is—that's not the point.) But not everything is the same; the sole difference is that the clear, colourless liquid that fills streams and oceans on Twin-Earth, that fishes swim in, that people put a little of in their Scotch, etc., has all the characteristics of water but a different chemical basis: instead of having the formula H_2O, it has different atomic constituents, and we'll call its formula XYZ (xantho-ytterbic zircothallium). Now, all the people on Earth have their exact duplicates on Twin-Earth, and their duplicates all do and say the same things as they do on Earth at the same time. So when Roger says, in English, "Yuck! That's water in this martini glass!" then at that same instant, his duplicate, Twin-Roger, says, in what sounds exactly like English, "Yuck! That's water in this martini glass!" But when Twin-Roger says "water" he's referring to XYZ, not H_2O.

Now, here are the intuitions we're supposed to have about this. Even though Roger and Twin-Roger are completely identical inside—have, in other words, the same brain configurations and the same psychology as each other at that moment (and at each moment of their identical lives) they nevertheless mean something different when they say "water." Hilary Putnam, who invented this argument, draws the conclusion that "meanings ain't in the head." They are a matter of what externals the words, and what's in the head, are related to—of the causal relation between externals and the word.[59]

Again, a critic can reply: that's not my intuition; it's rather that Roger and Twin-Roger mean the same thing by 'water', so meanings are in the head. Other critics react to this story by agreeing that Roger and Twin-Roger mean different things by 'water', but claim what you mean is a psychological matter, so conclude that Roger and Twin-Roger have different psychologies.

6. Where's Waldo?

Imagine that Waldo and Wendy are anaesthetised. Then each person's brain patterns—the complex arrangements of neural connections that record each person's memories—are analysed and recorded by a supercomputer. Then those patterns are wiped out from each brain, and then reprogrammed into the other body's brain. Now the person in the female body wakes up and remembers living in Waldo's house, being married to Waldo's wife, having had an appointment with a urologist about an enlarged prostate, and so on. That person is also quite surprised to see the female body in the mirror. Is the person in the female body Waldo or Wendy?

John Locke famously discussed a story of this sort (involving the "soul" of a cobbler who came to inhabit the body of a prince.[60] (Locke does not explain how this happened.) Many philosophers since have agreed with Locke's intuition that memories make the continuing person; so in our version, it's Waldo now in that female body. Note that calling those beliefs that are expressed by the person now in the female body "memories" begs the question (see the Glossary at the end of this book for an explanation of what begging the question is); your real memories are of things that happened to you. So the question we should ask about this story is: are those newly implanted beliefs about the past real memories or fakes? If your intuition is that post-operations, Waldo is in the female body, then the memories in the female body are Waldo's and real. And since Wendy is now inhabiting Waldo's former body, the memories in that body are Wendy's and real also.

If you have these intuitions, consider this story, with the same end point, but told slightly differently, aiming at pumping your intuitions in the other direction. Imagine that Waldo is told that he's going to be anaesthetized, and then all his memories are going to be erased from his brain. "Oh no!" says Waldo. "Amnesia!" "Don't feel so bad," says the mad doctor, "I'll put some other memories into your brain." "That's no better! That's worse!" says Waldo. Fake memories! I want my real ones!" "Well," says the doctor, "your real ones won't be destroyed. We're doing the same operation on Wendy, and programming your memories into her brain." "Still worse!" screams Waldo. "I don't want her to have my memories! I like those memories, and I don't like Wendy. I don't want her to get those memories!"

Has this variation on the story pumped your intuitions to the reverse?

CHAPTER 11

INFERENCE TO THE BEST EXPLANATION

THE BEST EXPLANATION

We next turn to a type of argument that uses a variety of reasoning familiar from everyday life. It argues that a hypothesis is true because it provides the best explanation for what is already known.

An example. You go to the fridge in the evening to get that carton of leftover kung-pao chicken for your dinner, but it's not there. What explains that? You come up with some guesses. Maybe your roommate came in late last night. (He has the tendency to raid the fridge when he does this.) Maybe burglars broke in while you were at work and stole it. Maybe you didn't put it in the fridge after dinner yesterday, but absent-mindedly put it in your sock drawer, or in the closet or somewhere. Maybe your mother came in during the day for an unannounced tidy-up, and threw it into the trash. You conclude that your roommate came in late last night. The other possible explanations seem too unlikely.

This sort of argument first gathers together a bunch of hypotheses which would explain what you know (that the kung-pao chicken isn't in the fridge); then picks the best among these.

> *Notice that this argument fits the definition of 'induction' given above, giving its conclusion probability. Sometimes, however, it's called 'abduction' instead. (But don't confuse this with being kidnapped by aliens on their flying saucer).*

Here's a complication. Suppose that in fact your roommate came in late last night. So your conclusion is true. It's also justified by the fact that the kung-pao chicken is not in the fridge. If knowledge is justified true belief, then you know your roommate came in. But suppose that your roommate didn't in fact eat the chicken, so his arrival doesn't explain the missing chicken, and your argument is defective. Do you really know that he came in? (This change makes the example similar to the Lucy-and-her-watch case above.)

Already we can see what might go wrong in this type of argument. First, maybe your list of explanatory hypotheses (I'll use the abbreviation 'EHS') doesn't include the real explanation. In that case, however, if you decide among the EHS you've thought of, you'll get the wrong answer. Suppose the real explanation for the missing kung-pao chicken is that you ate it all the other day and forgot you did. You reach the wrong conclusion.

So to guard against this, you must try to accumulate as many EHS as you can before you reach a conclusion, right? Well, no. With some imagination you can cook up an indefinitely large number of EHS which would explain the data. Here are some:

- Huge mutant horror-movie-style ants—big enough to open the fridge door—came in during the night and carried away the kung-pao chicken container.
- Hungry aliens from the planet Zarkon teletransported themselves into your fridge and ate it.
- The kung-pao chicken and its container contained a newly discovered substance that caused both to vaporize after a day in the fridge.
- An earthquake during the night caused the fridge door to open, and the kung-pao chicken container to fall out of the fridge and roll out the front door of your house, where it was grabbed and taken away by a passing raccoon.

But these are so implausible that you would immediately rule them out in the second stage of the argument, when you narrow down the list to the one you're going to believe. What you want to do, then, is to come up with a wide-ranging list of EHs, but not ridiculous ones.

And this leads to the obvious second problem: suppose you manage to get the EH on your list that really explains the data; but you reject it as less plausible than another one. This of course can happen, either because you misjudge plausibility, or because the right explanation really is one that anyone would rationally judge to be comparatively implausible. Strange things do happen.

Well, the next problem. Suppose that several EHs on the list look plausible. What then? Then perhaps you can subject some or all of them to empirical tests. Empirical tests can come in two types: those that can make an EH more likely—confirm it; and those that can make it less likely—disconfirm it.

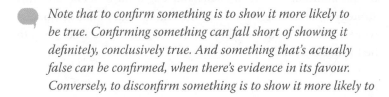

Note that to confirm something is to show it more likely to be true. Confirming something can fall short of showing it definitely, conclusively true. And something that's actually false can be confirmed, when there's evidence in its favour. Conversely, to disconfirm something is to show it more likely to be false, etc.

Here's an empirical test that can be confirmation. When your mother comes to tidy, she gets rid of that cache of empty beer bottles that you stored in a closet intending to do something about them some day. So if she's been in your apartment during the day, the beer bottles would be gone. You look in the closet, and the bottles are gone. This confirms—makes it more likely—that your mom has been here. But be careful: as always, this kind of inductive argument can give the wrong conclusion. Maybe those beer bottles had some other fate. And secondly: suppose your mom, as this evidence indicates, really was there tidying, but by that time something else had happened to the leftover kung-pao chicken. So while it's true that she came, that doesn't explain the missing food.

Disconfirmation, when available, can be more helpful. Same example, same EH: that mom did it; you look in the closet and the bottles are all there. So this disconfirms the EH that mom was there tidying—that is, it makes it less likely that she was there. (But only less likely, not completely impossible: maybe, uncharacteristically, she didn't clear away your bottle collection.) Maybe that's enough evidence to show she wasn't there; then you can rule out that EH. If you can rule out all the rest of the EHs except for one, then that gives you your conclusion: the only remaining EH is the one you accept. (It helps if, in addition, you have confirmation for that remaining EH.)

What we need here, putting it briefly, is the EH that best fits the data—the information we already have, and the information we can get from additional observations and experiments. But there's still another complication to be noted here. Suppose you make an observation that contradicts an EH you favour. It would seem always to be rational to doubt, or even dispose of, that EH. But there's another choice here that shouldn't be sneezed at: to doubt or even dispose of the information you thought you got from observation. This strategy is, of course, very often the telltale sign of bad reasoning: when what you want to believe in conflicts with the facts, then to hell with the facts!

Wholesale discarding of data that conflict with your favourite theory is paradigmatic bad science. But (weirdly) it has its defenders. The famous linguist Noam Chomsky proudly announced that he (and all the other great scientists!) have theories that are thoroughly refuted by the data, but "You just see that some ideas simply look right, and then you sort of put aside the data that refute them."[61]

But sometimes information from an observation is not all that certain, and it's more rational to locate the problem not with the EH, but rather with the observation. Of course, this has to be done very sparingly and reluctantly.

There's a story I heard in the university I used to work in about a science professor there whom I'll call Dr. X. Decades ago, Dr. X repeatedly got experimental measurements in his lab that appeared to conflict with well-established theory. After much additional investigation, he still couldn't figure out what had happened, but he finally concluded that there was something wrong with his instruments, and dropped the matter. A while later, another scientist got the same sort of data, but concluded instead that the theory was wrong. That was correct, and for this the other scientist won a Nobel Prize. The thing to note here is that what Dr. X did was good science.

THEORY

You may have noticed that there's a common type of reasoning in science that is a lot like the chicken example above: an inference to the best *theory*.

What's a theory? In everyday talk, if someone says "That's just a theory," what they mean is, *that's just a guess.* So before you check things out, in the kung-pao-chicken example, you look for some hypotheses, and when a plausible one occurs to you, you might say, "I think my roommate ate it, but that's just my theory." But science and philosophy use that word differently. A theory, first of all, is an explanation, but of a more complicated sort. A theoretical explanation characteristically explains a bunch of phenomena, not just one (as in the kung-pao-chicken case). So it has more general application; it's expected to yield some predictions about a variety of things we might observe in the future. It does this by proposing an account of the underlying structure of the general sorts of things under consideration, or what, in general, causes them, or what sort of basic nature they have, or what they're composed of.

Theories are usually more complicated systems of assertions than the simple factual EHs in the kung-pao-chicken example. Sometimes these may assert the existence of entities or processes that are not observed, maybe that cannot be observed.

So in science we have, for example:

- the heliocentric (sun at the centre) theory of the solar system, which explains the apparent motion of planets in the night sky
- cell theory, that explains the structure and functional basis of the parts of living things
- the atomic theory, that explains chemical and physical reactions of physical stuff

- plate tectonic theory that explains the location and the behaviour of earthquakes and volcanoes
- evolutionary theory that explains how the complex adaptations of organisms came to be

You'll notice that these theories are—at present—not mere guesses at all. Each of them is highly confirmed, supported by vast amounts of evidence, vastly superior to any alternatives (none of which is taken seriously any more), and believed by just about everyone with any scientific background to be accounts of the real world. But each of them started out (sometimes centuries ago) as something like educated guesses—EHs that needed the support of good inferences to the best explanation. And each got that support. But in every science there are, of course, EHs that are still just candidates for support—plausible hypotheses in competition with others to see which one works best—or even, just guesses.

OTHER CRITERIA FOR A GOOD EXPLANATION

What's going on in the argument to the best explanation is, as should now be evident, a pretty complicated (and, I should mention controversial) matter. But when the EH is not just a simple proposition, but a candidate for an explanatory theory, there are additional complications.

So far, the arguments for an EH have used two sorts of tests: the plausibility test (coherence with what's already believed), and empirical testing (confirmation or disconfirmation). But suppose that these tests aren't sufficient: that some EHs remain despite all this. Various proposals have been made about additional criteria for choosing, especially when the EHs involved are proposed theories.

- Degree of empirical content. Roughly speaking, the degree of empirical content a proposed theory has is the amount of information the theory conveys about the observable world. The more the better.

Related to this is:

- Potential. A theory is comparatively preferable which has the potential for the wider variety of predictions, and thus will be more testable. (A theory with more empirical content sometimes therefore offers more opportunities for empirical test.)
- Fecundity. A theory is better when it is applicable to a wider variety of cases, and when it generates more new ideas.

Here's another criterion, sometimes in conflict with the first three:

- Simplicity. A simpler theory is a better theory. A theory is simpler when, roughly speaking, it involves postulation of fewer unobserved objects, or requires simpler calculations for its predictions, or a smaller number of principles or suppositions.

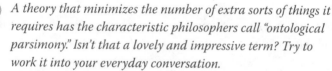

A theory that minimizes the number of extra sorts of things it requires has the characteristic philosophers call "ontological parsimony." Isn't that a lovely and impressive term? Try to work it into your everyday conversation.

The simplicity criterion for theory-worth is called "Ockham's Razor." It was named after the fourteenth-century English philosopher William of Ockham, who produced an influential statement of this principle (but was not the first to propose it). It's often supposed that it's called a "razor" because it shaves away unnecessary complications. 'Razor' has the same etymological root as 'eraser'; both come from a root meaning to scrape. That's because in pre-paper pre-pencil medieval times, one removed mistakes written in ink on vellum (animal skin) by scraping with a razor. "Ockham's eraser" would be a better name for the principle.

And lastly:

- Integration. The theory is preferable which is more integrated with the rest of contemporary knowledge. (This is a fancy, more general, version of the plausibility test mentioned above.)

These do seem to be factors that sometimes influence the way real scientists really do make choices among alternative theories. But, bearing in mind that the point of all this is *truth*, we might ask whether application of any of these criteria makes conclusions more likely to be true. Compare, in this respect, two additional factors that (unfortunately) figure in real-life science theory choice, and that are clearly quite unrelated to truth-seeking:

- Scientists are more likely to arrive at conclusions that are in accord with their socially produced perspectives, prejudices, political/religious/ideological commitments, and expectations of what will add to their career advancement, power, and influence.
- Scientists are more likely to choose an explanation that's more advantageous to the economic interests of the organization that's the source of their research funds.

Well, yes, that's how humans sometimes work. But if a scientist is really after truth....

How big an influence are these unfortunate factors on scientific conclusions? Some contemporary theorists argue that these matters dominate scientific procedure to such a degree that it's inappropriate to think of any conclusions as true. Some suggest we abandon the idea of objectivity altogether. See the section on Scientific Realism/Antirealism below.

PHILOSOPHICAL INFERENCES TO THE BEST THEORETICAL EXPLANATION: SOME EXAMPLES

Why have we been dwelling so long on explanation in science? Well, one of the jobs of philosophy is also to produce and assess theories. While philosophical explanations aren't normally empirical (and so the "degree of empirical content" criterion for a good theory might not apply), they can be assessed by much the same standards as are applied to best-explanation arguments in science. Here are some inferences to the best explanation in philosophy. See if you can detect some of the criteria for a good scientific explanation in each of these.

1. Tornado in a Junkyard

The application of the best-explanation argument that non-philosophers are probably most familiar with is an attempt to give evidence for the existence of God. The existence of certain aspects of the visible world—the usual example is the complex adaption of living things to their environment—has no better explanation, it's said, than supernatural design. An alternative EH is the random processes of nature, unguided by aims and intelligence. A memorable argument against the naturalistic EH was provided by the twentieth-century English astronomer Sir Fred Hoyle, who gave a "that's-like-arguing" objection, saying that the possibility that higher life forms could have been produced this way is comparable to the chance that "a tornado sweeping through a junk yard might assemble a Boeing 747 from the materials therein."[62]

 Hoyle did important groundbreaking work on the origin of stars, but he was also widely known for his loudly proclaimed crackpot views in other areas. He argued, for example, that flu epidemics were correlated with sunspots, and were caused by invasions of viruses from outer space; that petroleum deposits could not be formed from buried ancient organic matter; and that a famous Archaeopteryx (winged dinosaur) fossil was a fake. "I don't care what they think," said Hoyle. "It is better to be interesting and wrong than boring and right."[63]

Hoyle compares two proposed explanatory hypotheses: that the complexities of living things came about through intelligent design; the second is that such complexities arose suddenly, fully developed, as the result of a random mixing of their basic elements (this is the hugely improbable hypothesis that Hoyle is making fun of). But he's left another hypothesis off the list of possibilities: evolution, the account just about all biologists, and most educated people, believe today. This is, of course, the idea that complex organisms developed over a very long period of mutation and selection of the fittest, starting from extremely primitive combinations that might have arisen purely at random, and going through a huge number of mostly small inherited changes. Given that the evidence for this sort of evolution is overwhelming, this hypothesis is hugely probable, and the argument that intelligent design is the only good explanation loses all force.

 Yes, I know that you can find some people who think that evolution never happened, or could not have happened just through natural processes. No, I'm not going to treat their position seriously. The empirical superiority of the evolution hypothesis comes from fossil evidence of earlier forms of life, and from the structural/functional similarity of closely related organisms, pointing to development from a common ancestor. However, the apparent empirical superiority of the evolution hypothesis can be attacked by adding explanations of how all that empirical "evidence" might be discounted, explained away by ad hoc suppositions added to the intelligent design hypothesis. We'll see below why this is not sufficient to explain away fossils.

2. Ethical Theory

Like some theories in science, ethical theories attempt to explain the data in a particular area by means of an EH describing the underlying general structure of what's going on in that area—an EH that best explains the data. The data in ethics are our "ethical intuitions"— our feelings about the rightness or wrongness of particular actions. What sort of theory will explain and unify these intuitions? Is the moral worth of an action a matter of how much happiness it creates for everyone affected? Is it a matter simply of always respecting persons as ends in themselves, never as merely means? Is it a matter of its effects on human flourishing? You can easily find outlines of how these, and other, moral theories are supposed to work, and I'm not going to talk about that here. One thing very interesting about moral theory, however, is a matter we talked about above: sometimes it's rational to doubt the data, rather than to reject your favourite EH. For example, if you have an intuition about the morality of abortion (or capital punishment, or the existence of huge economic differences in society, or telling white lies, or raising animals for food), you might just abandon that intuition if you find that it conflicts with your most general moral principles—your moral theory. Some philosophers have commented on that peculiarity of philosophical moral explanation: that there's an extraordinary amount of give-and-take between data and theory. When they conflict, sometimes you modify the theory, but often you throw out the data. (This account of ethical theory is associated with influential work by John Rawls.[64] He named what he took to be the aim of ethical theory—the mutual adjustment of principles and intuitions—'reflective equilibrium'.)

3. Mind and Brain

There is a lot of inductive evidence that types of mental goings-on are correlated with types of brain events. But what some philosophers have proposed is the mind/brain identity theory—the idea that mental properties *are* physical properties. Opponents of this view—dualists—are willing to accept correlation, but insist that there are two different things here, that just always go together. If there were no other reason to choose between these two hypotheses, then simplicity (Ockham's razor) would be decisive, and we should choose the theory that postulates only one kind of stuff—the material—which then would be seen to underlie all sorts of processes, inside and outside of people.

But are these hypotheses equal in every other way? Dualists reply that they are not. What's mental cannot really be a type of physical event, because of evident differences between the two types of things. One difference is that mental events are representational—have "aboutness." A thought might be about Vienna, but a physical brain event—it's argued—cannot be. (Of course, this claim is controversial. Maybe what makes a brain event about Vienna is that it's connected through a long cause/effect chain to that city.) Another difference is that mental events have an experienced feeling: whatever is going on in your brain when you have the sense-experience of tasting a grapefruit, still there's *what it's like to you*. (The Zombie thought experiment, discussed above, is supposed to illustrate the difference between a physical state and a mental one, when we are urged to think about beings with one but not the other.) No physical process can have this experiential aspect, they argue.

Well, as you can imagine, we've just scratched the surface of this debate.

4. The External World (Again)

Is there a world external to our perceptions? Yes, there is, dammit, aargh. But there's a long philosophical tradition of looking for a defence of this view (which we'll call realism about the external world) against alternative sceptical hypotheses.

> *The word 'realism' here (and below) does not carry its ordinary-language implication of calculating rationality or practicality as opposed to sentimentality or motivation by abstract principle. In philosophical jargon, "realism" applies to a variety of positions affirming the independence of externals independent of our way of seeing them, or talking or thinking about them.*

We've already talked about the attempt to defend this realism on the grounds that it's the common-sense view; but here we'll now look at a different sort of defence: in a nutshell, that the existence of an external world independent of our minds, language, practice, etc.— an external world pretty much, *in some respects*, like the way we experience it—is the best explanation for our experience.

> *I say "in some respects" because one common modern version of realism is that matter with location and shape and mass is out there, and that other features we seem to sense in the external world, such as flavours, colours, odours, are subjective: caused by the more basic physical and chemical properties of externals. (Remember the tree falling in the forest?)*

The best-explanation argument compares alternative EHs. A very well-known alternative EH was thought up by Descartes: in his *Meditations*, he considers the possibility that all his experience is produced by an "evil genius" (sometimes translated "evil demon")—a powerful and malevolent being who produces all those beliefs and experiences in him, so that he is mistaken even about the most common-sense beliefs and the most obvious everyday perceptions. A more modern science-fictionny version of this hypothesis is Hilary Putnam's "brain-in-a-vat" supposition:[65] a mad super-scientist has removed your brain at birth and immersed it in a nutritive solution in a vat in his laboratory, where it is connected to a supercomputer that feeds in all that "sensory" information about the appearance of your hands, your car, trees, the kung-pao chicken in your refrigerator, etc.; all this, then, is hallucination.

You might be reminded of the movie The Matrix, *and there actually is a connection between the movie and Putnam. He said that his chapter on brains in vats "had basically the same scenario as* The Matrix *does....I was not aware that the producers of* The Matrix *had read my work. It seemed possible that they came on this idea by themselves; but, in fact, before* The Matrix II *was released, I was approached and asked whether I was willing for my chapter to be listed in references on the* Matrix II *website. I gave my permission."*[66]

Neither Descartes nor Putnam deploys the inference to the best explanation against their sceptical hypotheses. Never mind what their arguments are: think about how the best-explanation argument works here.

First, notice how these two hypotheses are set up. Each of them is, importantly, empirically equivalent with the hypothesis that there is a real external world that is more or less the way it seems. That is to say: no observation or experiment you could do could test whether there's really an external world there, or on the contrary you're just being manipulated by an evil demon or by a mad scientist.

But nevertheless, it's sometimes argued, the external world hypothesis is the better explanation. Notice the pervasive regularities in your experience. For example: What look like oranges also *always* smell like, feel like, and taste like oranges. What look like your shoes always feel right when you (apparently) put them on your feet. And so on. In order to achieve these and countless other regularities,

Descartes's evil genius or Putnam's mad scientist would have to provide extremely regular correlations and repetitions among the hallucinations they're feeding into you. Why are they doing this? All this regularity seems wholly arbitrary, inexplicable, and improbable. (If you were that genius/scientist, would you go to the huge extra effort of regularizing the hallucinations you were producing?) But much simpler is the explanation that there really are oranges with that look, that smell, that taste, and that feel, *out there*. It's because it's a real orange combining all these real characteristics that your orange-experiences are so regular. (And shoe-experiences, etc.) That there's an external world out there with its own laws making things endure when unobserved, and behave regularly, is by far the better—simpler—explanation.

Well, so it's claimed. But is it really simpler? A real physical world involves countless different particular objects and kinds of objects, with countless regularities and correlations. Descartes's and Putnam's imaginary worlds are in one way much simpler, in that all they need is a nasty manipulator (plus some hardware in Putnam's scientist's laboratory). (There's a general problem here, which we'll go no further into, about what's a "simpler" explanation. And of course, there's also the problem already mentioned about why simplicity is supposed to be related to truth.

5. The Five Minute Hypothesis

This is a similar sort of sceptical hypothesis, but a bit less widely known, and somewhat more amusing: that the world was created five minutes ago. Of course, there appears to be abundant evidence against this: you remember the movie you saw last week; your socks have holes in them as if they were years old; on your computer's hard disc are thousands of photographs with dates from the past, showing people that look younger. The five minute hypothesis accommodates all this: it's all a fraud. The world was created five minutes ago complete with what you take to be all sorts of evidence, including your memories (and those of others who agree with you), and a whole lot of fake antiques.

Bertrand Russell invented this story, published in one of his books in 1921.[67]

Oops, I mean the story is in a book that appeared five minutes ago, complete with a title page that says "©1921."

In the book he says there is no "logical impossibility" in this story. He means that it isn't self-contradictory; and we can add that it's empirically equivalent to the alternative realistic hypothesis. Russell says, "I am not here suggesting that the non-existence of the past should be entertained as a serious hypothesis. Like all sceptical hypotheses, it is logically tenable but uninteresting." No, he's wrong: it's interesting, not because it's tempting to believe, but because it apparently needs to be shown false by argument, and it's not obvious how to do that.

Here's something else interesting about this hypothesis. A version of this (which we'll call the '6,000 year hypothesis') is actually believed by significant portions of the population, including some people not obviously insane. Many religious people believe that the Old Testament is literally true. From what it says there, the date of creation can be calculated, and a seventeenth-century Irish bishop named James Ussher did this. Ussher announced that the world began at 6 p.m. on Saturday, October 22, 4004 BCE. (He doesn't identify the time zone in which it was 6 p.m.)[68]

 The noted twentieth-century evolutionary biologist, palaeontologist, and historian of science Stephen Jay Gould urges us not to mock Ussher's chronology. It is, Gould says, "an honorable effort for its time and ... our usual ridicule only records a lamentable small-mindedness based on mistaken use of present criteria to judge a distant and different past." But, of course, he doesn't think it's an alternative hypothesis nowadays worth considering.

Other calculations come close to this, including those by the great scientists Johannes Kepler (his suggestion: 3992 BCE) and Isaac Newton (his estimate: c. 4000 BCE). To accommodate this sort of timetable, religious thinkers had to deal with the fossil remains of dinosaurs and other extinct organisms, apparently very long gone. Sometimes they claimed that the fossils were remains of animals that died in the biblical flood (c. 2350 BCE), but advances in geology appeared to show that what was dug up was millions of years old. Those who hung on to a literal reading of the Bible had an answer: all these fossils are fake antiques, created no more than a few thousand years ago, but artificially decorated with the signs of being much older (probably put there to test our faith). This is the official position of some large religious groups today.

You should note that Russell's five minute hypothesis and Ussher's 6,000 year hypothesis both have been shielded from refutation by empirical evidence; this makes the two of them and the current view of science (which puts the origin of the universe at approximately 14 billion years ago) empirically equivalent: all three of them (in different ways) account for what seems to be evidence about the past. This is where the simplicity criterion for the best explanation might come into play. The Russell and the Ussher hypotheses are loaded with all sorts of ad hoc assumptions to account for what seems like evidence of a more distant past; the idea that a more distant past really did exist is maybe the simplest of the three hypotheses, and thus the best of them.

6. Scientific Realism/Antirealism

Scientific realism is the position that the real world really does have the properties modern science attributes to it. How can this be controversial? Well, consider scientific explanation. As we've seen, choosing the explanation for observed phenomena involves some fairly subjective matters. First, you have to compile a list of EHS, and maybe you leave the right one out. Then you have to choose among the hypotheses you can think of, and of course, you may choose the wrong one. Empirical evidence may not help, because, as we've seen with the sceptical hypotheses we've looked at, there are always ways of adding ad hoc additional suppositions to make any hypothesis consistent with the evidence. When two hypotheses are equally consistent with all the evidence, and there's no way to design an experiment which will choose between them—that is, when they're empirically equivalent—then the choice is based on non-empirical matters such as simplicity; and we've seen that which of two hypotheses is simpler is a debatable matter, and, anyway, that the connection between simplicity and truth is obscure. And there's a further reason to doubt that current science matches reality: the history of science shows that explanations are accepted for a while, then rejected in favour of others, which are in turn themselves rejected, and so on. Nothing lasts; all is flux.

> *This doesn't mean that everything is fluxed up. 'Flux' means flow. That everything is flux—change—was the view of the ancient Greek philosopher Heraclitus (c. 500 BCE). He's the guy that said you can't step into the same river twice, because the water is always different. (He didn't actually mean that the Nile then wasn't the same river as was there earlier—that nothing remains the same over time. He meant that it's a more complicated situation than just the same stuff.)*

And furthermore, there are examples of scientific fraud, and of influence from funding sources, personal ideology and prejudice, and so on. So why believe the current scientific orthodoxy? What all this adds up to is that it's not all that implausible to think that the scientific explanations we've settled on at present are not very likely to be true. Scientific antirealism is unlike antirealism about the external world or the past, in that you don't have to be crazy or super-religious to believe it.

But we'll look at just one argument for scientific realism about explanations: the "no miracles" argument, named after Hilary Putnam's claim that realism "is the only philosophy that doesn't make the success of science a miracle."[69] This is a version of the inference to the best explanation. The antirealist view, that our best science probably has little to do with reality, would make it highly unlikely that our scientific explanations ever worked: it would be a miracle if a rocket we built ever reached the moon, or if a vaccine prevented a disease, or if a bridge didn't collapse.

Interestingly, both the realist and the antirealist are relying on the history of science for these arguments: the antirealist cites the large number of historical scientific failures, and the realist on the large number of scientific successes. Are they reading different history books?

But another question we might raise here is this. The no-miracles argument is an inference to the best explanation. But the inference to the best explanation is central to the methodology of science, and it's exactly the truth-revealing potential of this methodology that is being questioned by the antirealists. So what we have here appears to be a kind of circular reasoning: it's using an inference to the best explanation to prove the truth-revealing power of the inference to the best explanation. In general, if prejudice, etc., determines the outcome of all of everyone's reasoning, then of course that reasoning will conclude that preferred scientific practice reveals truth, and of course that conclusion will be utterly untrustworthy.

This is a very serious problem, not just a little paradoxical quirk. REASON CAN'T DEFEND ITSELF. So is all that's left a matter of which group has the political power to enforce their views? Aw, Jeez.

7. The Problem of Induction

This problem has been bothering philosophers since it was revealed by David Hume in the eighteenth century. Here's the problem. Induction (of one sort, anyway, called *induction by enumeration*) uses past observed regularities to predict the future, relying on the principle (in Hume's words) that "instances of which we have had no experience resemble those of which we have had experience."[70] But what warrant is there for this principle? To claim that it has served us well in the past, so it's likely to continue to be useful is—again— apparently circular, using a principle of reasoning to justify itself.

D.M. Armstrong has produced an interesting best-explanation argument for the conclusion that induction is reliable.[71] He argues that the best explanation for observed regularities is that they are the result of objective natural necessities—real external mind-independent laws of nature; and these laws enable predictions about future observations. I'll leave it to you to try to determine if this, in a more complicated way, commits the kind of circularity Hume warned against.

8. Ethical Realism/Antirealism

Ethical realism is the view that there are external mind- and culture-independent ethical facts. Ethical antirealism is, of course, the view that there aren't any such facts: there are only culturally invented and enforced rules, and individual pro- and con-attitudes. You might expect an inference to the best explanation, parallel to the one just discussed above, in support of ethical realism. But here, interestingly, an inference to the best explanation is used in favour of the antirealist position.

The fact from which this argument begins is that there exists at the present time, and through history, widespread moral disagreement between individuals and between cultures. These disagreements haven't been settled by empirical means, or by argument. Compare this to science, or to common-sense and perceptual beliefs, where there's some disagreement, of course, but not anywhere near as much. Sensible people show almost complete agreements about ordinary facts; and science, while manifesting a historical diversity of opinion, has worked toward a remarkable convergence about the basics. In both cases, there are widely agreed-on and often conclusive methods for resolving disagreements, whereas disagreements in ethical positions don't go away, and they resist any method for rational resolution. The best explanation of this is that there aren't any facts to be known in ethics. There are just individual feelings, and (varying) social customs. That's ethical antirealism.

There are several points at which critics attack this argument. They claim, for one thing, that it exaggerates the extent of ethical disagreement. Some disagreements in what ought to be done are the result different beliefs about non-moral facts: for example, if we disagree about whether global warming is caused by additional atmospheric CO_2, then we'll disagree about whether countries should embark on expensive carbon-reduction schemes. Some disagreements are based on differences in people's situation: various practices that we'd find immoral might be acceptable (for example) in a culture living in conditions of extreme hardship. And maybe there is a core of moral agreement among all sensible people. And maybe the remaining disagreements aren't intractable, but could eventually be solved by discussion among people willing to try. Ethics, after all, is hard: it takes specialized training to do well (like science), so it's no wonder that a lot of people get things wrong.

So the question is: even considering all these objections, is ethical disagreement still so different from other sorts of disagreement that we should conclude that there are no real ethical facts?

AFTERWORD

Philosophy is the oldest intellectual discipline there is. In about 500 BCE, while my ancestors, and probably yours, were painting themselves blue, and thinking about nothing but sex and food and killing everyone in the clan next door, Thales, in Greece, was doing philosophy. That's how old it is in the Western tradition, and older in the Eastern.

Because it has been going on for so long, inside so many different cultures and traditions, and because it is home to just about any sort of very general thought that hasn't relocated to another discipline, it is remarkably diverse in subject matter and methodology.

 A lot of what once was considered philosophy has been relocated. Aristotle's work included writing on geology, physics, optics, biology, psychology, and a number of other sciences. Newton's great three-volume work on physics was called Philosophiae Naturalis Principia Mathematica—*Latin for Mathematical Principles of Natural Philosophy—but now, of course, it's physics. Bertrand Russell, who was a pessimist about the possibility of real knowledge in what's left in philosophy, said "[a]s soon as definite knowledge concerning any subject becomes possible, this subject ceases to be called philosophy, and becomes a separate science."*[72]

It's even a matter of some debate exactly what philosophy is supposed to be doing. The answer is that (unlike other areas) it's doing a huge variety of things, in all sorts of different ways.

And what that means is that any account of what's going on in the field, with advice about how to do it, has a point of view that some philosophers will disagree with. Of course! Philosophy of philosophy is another branch of philosophy, and as such it includes opposing viewpoints; and any work in that area must take some sides. You must already have noticed that this book is opinionated. I've made some efforts (in accord with my own advice in here) (usually) to be fair, but it wouldn't be hard to find some philosophers who would tell you that their idea of what they're doing, and of what their students should be doing, is rather different from the views in here. That's okay! In fact, that's good! Let there be controversy!

But in any case, the perspectives in here are at least widely shared among today's philosophers; so my advice won't lead you very far astray as a student in the field. I hope what I've said presents philosophizing as a fascinating and worthwhile activity, and helps you do it better.

APPENDIX 1

SOME VERY BRIEF SUGGESTIONS ABOUT FURTHER READING

I'm not completely sure that reading books about "critical think-ing" and the fallacies, or about the basics of inductive or deductive logic, will be a great deal of practical use. But if you're interested, there are hundreds of these books, and it won't be hard to find some. More useful, perhaps, will be books of practical advice on writing essays, especially argumentative ones. Those specifically about phil-osophical writing are not common—you're more likely to find them directed toward writing about literature, or about humanities sub-jects in general.

But I will recommend a particular book about philosophical methodology: *An Introduction to Philosophical Methods* by Chris Daly (Peterborough, ON: Broadview Press, 2010). It's a serious and penetrating exploration of the structures and presuppositions and possible justifications of philosophical methodologies, so it's a phil-osophical treatise, not a book of practical advice. It's philosophy of philosophy.

APPENDIX 2

FORMS FOR FOOTNOTES AND BIBLIOGRAPHY[73]

ABOUT CHICAGO STYLE

The University of Chicago's massively comprehensive *Chicago Manual of Style* (16th edition, 2010), provides full information on two documentation systems: an author/date system of citation that is similar to APA (American Psychological Association) Style, and a traditional foot- or endnoting system. The latter, which this book refers to as Chicago Style, and which is often used in the history and philosophy disciplines, is outlined below.

In the pages that follow, information about electronic sources has been presented in an integrated fashion, with information about referencing hard copies of print sources presented alongside information about referencing online versions. General guidelines covering entries for online sources are as follows. Begin each note and bibliography entry for an electronic source as you would for a non-electronic source, including all relevant publication information that the source makes available. Then provide either the website's URL, followed by the usual end punctuation for the note or entry, or, if available, the source's digital object identifier (DOI): a string of numbers, letters, and punctuation, beginning with 10, usually located on the first or copyright page. If both a URL and DOI are available, provide only the latter; DOIs are preferred because they are stable links to sources, whereas URLs are often not permanent. If you need to break a URL or DOI over two or more lines, do not insert any hyphens at the break point; instead, break after a colon or double slash or before other marks of punctuation. Note that (unlike MLA

[Modern Language Association] Style), Chicago Style does not put angle brackets around URLS. Except when there is no publication or modification date available, Chicago Style does not require the addition of access dates for online material, but your instructors may wish you to include them. If so, put them after the URL or DOI, after the word *accessed*.

1. Notes

The basic principle of Chicago Style is to create a note each time one cites a source. The note can appear at the foot of the page on which the citation is made, or it can be part of a separate list, titled *Notes*, situated at the end of the essay and before the bibliography. For both foot- and endnotes, a superscript number in the text points to the relevant note:

> Bonnycastle refers to "the true and lively spirit of opposition" with which Marxist literary criticism invigorates the discipline.[1]

The superscript number [1] here is linked to the information provided where the same number appears at either the foot of the page or in the list of notes at the end of the main text of the paper:

> 1.   Stephen Bonnycastle, *In Search of Authority: An Introductory Guide to Literary Theory*, 3rd ed. (Peterborough, ON: Broadview Press, 2007), 204.

Notice that the author's name is in the normal order, elements of the note are separated by commas, publication information is in parentheses, and the first line of the note is indented. The note ends with a page number for the citation.

In addition, all works cited, as well as works that have been consulted but are not cited in the body of your essay, must be included in an alphabetically arranged list, titled *Bibliography*, that appears at the end of the essay. The entry there would in this case be as follows:

> Bonnycastle, Stephen. *In Search of Authority: An Introductory Guide to Literary Theory*. 3rd ed. Peterborough, ON: Broadview Press, 2007.

In the entry in the bibliography, notice that the author's name is inverted, elements of the entry are separated by periods, no parentheses are placed around the publication information. Also, the entry is given a hanging indent: the first line is flush with the left-hand margin, and subsequent lines are indented. Notice as well that the province or state of publication is included in both notes and bibliography entries if the city of publication is not widely known.

In the various examples that follow, note formats and bibliography entry formats for each kind of source are shown together.

2. Titles: Italics/Quotation Marks

Notice in the above example that both the title and the subtitle are in italics. Titles of short works (such as articles, poems, and short stories) should be put in quotation marks. In all titles key words should be capitalized.

3. Multiple References to the Same Work

For later references to an already-cited source, use the author's last name, title (in shortened form if it is over four words long), and page number only.

1. Bonnycastle, *In Search of Authority*, 28.

If successive references are to the same work, use ibid. (an abbreviation of the Latin *ibidem*, meaning *in the same place*) instead of repeating information that appears in the previous note.

1. Sean Carver, "The Economic Foundations for Unrest in East Timor, 1970–1995," *Journal of Economic History* 21, no. 2 (2011): 103.
2. Ibid., 109.
3. Ibid., 111.
4. Jennifer Riley, "East Timor in the Pre-Independence Years," *Asian History Online* 11, no. 4 (2012): par. 18, http:// www.aho.ubc.edu/ prs/text-only/issue.45/16.3jr.txt.
5. Ibid., par. 24.

Carver, Sean. "The Economic Foundations for Unrest in East Timor, 1970–1995." *Journal of Economic History* 21, no. 2 (2011): 100–121.

Riley, Jennifer. "East Timor in the Pre-Independence Years." *Asian History Online* 11, no. 4 (2012). http://www.aho.ubc.edu/prs/text-only/issue.45/16.3jr.txt.

4. Page Number or Date Unavailable

If an Internet document cited is in PDF format, the page numbers are stable and may be cited in the same way that one would the pages of a printed book or journal article. Many Internet page numbers are unstable, however, and many more lack page numbers. Instead, provide a section number, paragraph number, or other identifier if available.

2.   Hanif Bhabha, "Family Life in 1840s Virginia," *Southern History Web Archives* 45, no. 3 (2013): par. 14. http:// shweb.ut.edu/history/american.nineteenthc/bhabha.html (accessed March 3, 2009).

Bhabha, Hanif. "Family Life in 1840s Virginia." *Southern History Web Archives* 45, no. 3 (2013). http://shweb.ut.edu/history/american.nineteenthc/bhabha.html.

If you are citing longer texts from electronic versions, and counting paragraph numbers is impracticable, chapter references may be more appropriate. For example, if the online Gutenberg edition of Darwin's *On the Origin of Species* were being cited, the citation would be as follows:

Darwin refers to the core of his theory as an "ineluctable principle."[1]

1.   Charles Darwin, *On the Origin of Species* (1856; Project Gutenberg, 2001), chap. 26, http://www.gutenberg.darwin.origin.frrp.ch26.html.

Darwin, Charles. *On the Origin of Species.* 1856. Project Gutenberg, 2001. http://www.gutenberg.darwin.origin.frrp.ch26.html.

Students should be cautioned that online editions of older or classic works are often unreliable; typically there are far more typos and other errors in online versions of literary texts than there are in print versions.

When there is no date for a source, include n.d., as in the first example below. When there is no date for an online source, include your access date.

1. Thomas Gray, *Gray's Letters*, vol. 1 (London: John Sharpe, n.d.), 60.
2. Don LePan, *Skyscraper Art*, http://www.donlepan.com/Skyscraper_Art.html (accessed February 10, 2013).

Gray, Thomas. *Gray's Letters*. Vol. 1. London: John Sharpe, n. d.
LePan, Don. *Skyscraper Art*. http://www.donlepan.com/Skyscraper_Art. html (accessed February 10, 2013).

5. Two or More Dates for a Work

Note that in the Darwin example above both the date of the original publication and the date of the modern edition are provided. If you are citing work in a form that has been revised by the author, however, you should cite the date of the revised publication, not the original.

1. Eric Foner, *Free Soil, Free Labor, Free Men: A Study of Antebellum America*, rev. ed. (New York: Oxford University Press, 1999), 178.

Foner, Eric. *Free Soil, Free Labor, Free Men: A Study of Antebellum America*. Rev. ed. New York: Oxford University Press, 1999.

6. Two or Three Authors

If there are two or three authors, they should be identified as follows in the footnote and in the bibliography. Pay attention to where commas do and do not appear, and note that in the bibliography entry, only the first author's name is inverted. Put the names of the authors in the order in which they appear in the work itself.

4. Eric Alderman and Mark Green, *Tony Blair and the Rise of New Labour* (London: Cassell, 2002), 180.

Alderman, Eric, and Mark Green. *Tony Blair and the Rise of New Labour*. London: Cassell, 2002.

7. Four or More Authors

In the footnote name only the first author, and use the phrase et al., an abbreviation of the Latin et alii, meaning and others. In the bibliography name all authors, as below:

11. Victoria Fromkin et al., *An Introduction to Language*, 4th Canadian ed. (Toronto: Nelson, 2010), 113.

Fromkin, Victoria, Robert Rodman, Nina Hyams, and Kirsten M. Hummel. *An Introduction to Language*. 4th Canadian ed. Toronto: Nelson, 2010.

8. Author Unknown/Corporate Author/Government Document

Identify by the corporate author if known, and otherwise by the title of the work. Unsigned newspaper articles or dictionary and encyclopedia entries are usually not listed in the bibliography. In notes, unsigned dictionary or encyclopedia entries are identified by the title of the reference work, e.g., *Columbia Encyclopedia*, and unsigned newspaper articles are listed by the title of the article in footnotes but by the title of the newspaper in the bibliography. Ignore initial articles (the, a, an) when alphabetizing.

6. *National Hockey League Guide, 1966–67* (Toronto: National Hockey League, 1966), 77.
7. "Argentina's President Calls on UK Prime Minister to Relinquish Control of Falkland Islands," *Vancouver Sun*, January 3, 2013, A9.
8. Broadview Press, "Questions and Answers about Book Pricing," Broadview Press, http://www.broadviewpress.com/bookpricing. asp?inc=bookpricing (accessed January 18, 2013).
9. Commonwealth of Massachusetts, *Records of the Transportation Inquiry, 2004* (Boston: Massachusetts Publishing Office, 2005), 488.
10. *Columbia Encyclopedia*, "Ecuador," http://bartleby.com.columbia. txt.acc.html (accessed February 4, 2013).
11. U.S. Congress. House Committee on Ways and Means, Subcommittee on Trade, *Free Trade Area of the Americas: Hearings*, 105th Cong., 1st sess., July 22, 1997, Hearing Print 105–32, 160, http://www. waysandmeans.house.gov/hearings.asp (accessed January 22, 2013).

Following are the bibliography entries for the preceding notes (notice that, because unsigned newspaper articles and articles from well-known reference works are not usually included in Chicago Style bibliographies, the *Vancouver Sun* and *Columbia Encyclopedia* articles are not included):

Broadview Press. "Questions and Answers about Book Pricing." Broadview Press. http://www.broadviewpress.com/bookpricing. asp?inc=bookpricing (accessed January 18, 2013).

Commonwealth of Massachusetts. *Records of the Transportation Inquiry, 2004.* Boston: Massachusetts Publishing Office, 2005.

National Hockey League Guide, 1966–67. Toronto: National Hockey League, 1966.

U.S. Congress. House Committee on Ways and Means. Subcommittee on Trade. *Free Trade Area of the Americas: Hearing before the Subcommittee on Trade.* 105th Cong., 1st sess., July 22, 1997. Hearing Print 105–32. http:// www.waysandmeans.house.gov/ hearings.asp (accessed January 22, 2013).

9. Works from a Collection of Readings or Anthology

In the citation for a work in an anthology or collection of essays, use the name of the author of the work you are citing. If the work is reprinted in one source but was first published elsewhere, include the details of the original publication in the bibliography.

6. Eric Hobsbawm, "Peasant Land Occupations," in *Uncommon People: Resistance and Rebellion* (London: Weidenfeld & Nicolson, 1998), 167.

7. Frederic W. Gleach, "Controlled Speculation: Interpreting the Saga of Pocahontas and Captain John Smith," in *Reading Beyond Words: Contexts for Native History*, 2nd ed., ed. Jennifer Brown and Elizabeth Vibert (Peterborough, ON: Broadview Press, 2003), 43.

Gleach, Frederic W. "Controlled Speculation: Interpreting the Saga of Pocahontas and Captain John Smith." In *Reading Beyond Words: Contexts for Native History*, 2nd ed., edited by Jennifer Brown and Elizabeth Vibert, 39–74. Peterborough, ON: Broadview Press, 2003.

Hobsbawm, Eric. "Peasant Land Occupations." In *Uncommon People: Resistance and Rebellion*, 166–90. London: Weidenfeld & Nicolson, 1998. Originally published in *Past and Present* 62 (1974): 120–52.

10. Indirect Source

If you are citing a source from a reference other than the source itself, you should include information about both sources, supplying as much information as you are able to about the original source.

> In de Beauvoir's famous phrase, "one is not born a woman, one becomes one."[1]

1. Simone de Beauvoir, *The Second Sex* (London: Heinemann, 1966), 44, quoted in Ann Levey, "Feminist Philosophy Today," *Philosophy Now*, par. 8, http://www.ucalgary.ca.philosophy.nowsite675.html (accessed February 4, 2013).

de Beauvoir, Simone. *The Second Sex*. London: Heinemann, 1966. Quoted in Ann Levey, "Feminist Philosophy Today," *Philosophy Now*, http://www.ucalgary.ca.philosophy.nowsite675.html (accessed February 4, 2013).

11. Two or More Works by the Same Author

After the first entry in the bibliography, use three hyphens for subsequent entries of works by the same author (rather than repeat the author's name). Entries for multiple works by the same author are normally arranged alphabetically by title.

Menand, Louis. "Bad Comma: Lynne Truss's Strange Grammar." *The New Yorker*, June 28, 2004. http://www.newyorker.com/critics/books/?040628crbo_books1.
———. *The Metaphysical Club: A Story of Ideas in America*. New York: Knopf, 2002.

12. Edited Works

Entries for edited works include the abbreviation *ed.* or *eds*. Note that when *ed.* appears after a title, it means "edited by."

5. Brian Gross, ed., *New Approaches to Environmental Politics: A Survey* (New York: Duckworth, 2004), 177.
6. Mary Shelley, *Frankenstein*, 2nd ed., ed. Lorne Macdonald and Kathleen Scherf, Broadview Editions (1818; Peterborough, ON: Broadview Press, 2001), 89.

Gross, Brian, ed. *New Approaches to Environmental Politics: A Survey.*
New York: Duckworth, 2004.
Shelley, Mary. *Frankenstein.* 2nd ed. Edited by Lorne Macdonald
and Kathleen Scherf. Broadview Editions. Peterborough, ON:
Broadview Press, 2001. First published in 1818.

13. Translated Works

The name of the translator follows the work's title. Notice that, in
the example below, the work's author is unknown; begin with the
author's name if it is known.

1. *Beowulf,* trans. R.M. Liuzza, 2nd ed. (Peterborough, ON: Broadview
   Press, 2012), 91.
2. Franz Kafka, "A Hunger Artist," *The Metamorphosis and Other
   Stories,* trans. Ian Johnston (Peterborough, ON: Broadview Press,
   2015), 112.

Beowulf. Translated by R.M. Liuzza. 2nd ed. Peterborough, ON:
Broadview Press, 2012.
Kafka, Franz. "A Hunger Artist." *The Metamorphosis and Other Stories.*
Translated by Ian Johnston. Peterborough, ON: Broadview Press,
2015.

14. E-Books

Electronic books come in several formats. The first of the two sample
citations below is for a book found online; the second is for a book
downloaded onto an e-reader.

4. Mary Roberts Rinehart, *Tish* (1916; Project Gutenberg,
   2005), chap. 2, http://www.gutenberg.org/catalog/world/
   readfile?fk_files=1452441.
5. Lao Tzu, *Tao Te Ching: A Book about the Way and the Power of the
   Way,* trans. Ursula K. Le Guin (Boston: Shambhala, 2011), iBook
   Reader e-book, verse 12.

Lao Tzu. *Tao Te Ching: A Book about the Way and the Power of the Way.*
Translated by Ursula K. Le Guin. Boston: Shambhala, 2011. iBook
Reader e-book.
Rinehart, Mary Roberts. *Tish.* 1916. Project Gutenberg, 2005. http://
www.gutenberg.org/catalog/world/readfile?fk_files=1452441.

15. Magazine Articles

The titles of articles appear in quotation marks. The page range should appear in the bibliography if it is known. (This will not always be possible if the source is an electronic version.) If no authorship is attributed, list the title of the article as the "author" in the footnote, and the magazine title as the "author" in the bibliography. Do not include page numbers for online articles.

2. Alan Dyer, "The End of the World...Again," *SkyNews*, November/December 2012, 38.

3. "The Rise of the Yuan: Turning from Green to Red," *Economist*, October 20, 2012, 68.

4. Wendell Steavenson, "Two Revolutions: Women in the New Egypt," *The New Yorker*, November 12, 2012, http://www.newyorker.com/reporting/2012/11/12/121112fa_fact_steavenson.

Dyer, Alan. "The End of the World...Again." *SkyNews*, November/December 2012, 38–39. *Economist*. "The Rise of the Yuan: Turning from Green to Red." October 20, 2012, 67–68.

Steavenson, Wendell. "Two Revolutions: Women in the New Egypt." *The New Yorker*, November 12, 2012. http://www.newyorker.com/reporting/2012/11/12/121112fa_fact_steavenson.

16. Newspaper Articles

The basic principles to follow with newspaper articles or editorials are the same as with magazine articles (see above). Give page numbers in the note if your source is a hard copy rather than an electronic version, but indicate section designation alone in the bibliography entry.

1. Konrad Yakabuski, "Many Looking for Meaning in Vice-Presidential Debate," *The Globe and Mail*, October 12, 2012, A3.

2. Claudia La Rocco, "Where Chekhov Meets Christopher Walken," *The New York Times*, January 2, 2013, http://theater.nytimes.com/2013/01/03/theater/reviews/there-there-by-kristen-kosmas-at-the-chocolate-factory.html?ref=theater&_r=0.

La Rocco, Claudia. "Where Chekhov Meets Christopher Walken." *The New York Times*, January 2, 2013, http://theater.nytimes.com/2013/

01/03/theater/reviews/there-there-by-kristen-kosmas-at-the-chocolate-factory.html?ref=theater&_r=0.

Yakabuski, Konrad. "Many Looking for Meaning in Vice-Presidential Debate." *The Globe and Mail*, October 12, 2012, sec. A.

17. Journal Articles

The basic principles are the same as with magazine articles, but volume number, and issue number after no. (if the journal is published more than once a year), should be included as well as the date. Give page numbers where available. For online journal articles, provide the DOI, if available, rather than the URL.

1.   Paul Barker, "The Impact of Class Size on the Classroom Behavior of Special Needs Students: A Longitudinal Study," *Educational Quarterly* 25, no. 4 (2004): 88.

2.   Maciel Santos and Ana Guedes, "The Profitability of Slave Labor and the 'Time' Effect," *African Economic History* 36 (2008): 23.

3.   Thomas Hurka, "Virtuous Act, Virtuous Dispositions," *Analysis* 66, no. 1 (2006): 72.

4.   Ruth Groenhout, "The 'Brain Drain' Problem: Migrating Medical Professionals and Global Health Care," *International Journal of Feminist Approaches to Bioethics* 5, no. 1 (2012): 17, doi: 10.2979/intjfemappbio.5.1.1.

Barker, Paul. "The Impact of Class Size on the Classroom Behavior of Special Needs Students: A Longitudinal Study." *Educational Quarterly* 25, no. 4 (2004): 87–99.

Groenhout, Ruth. "The 'Brain Drain' Problem: Migrating Medical Professionals and Global Health Care." *International Journal of Feminist Approaches to Bioethics* 5, no. 1 (2012): 1–24, doi: 10.2979/intjfemappbio.5.1.1.

Hurka, Thomas. "Virtuous Act, Virtuous Dispositions." *Analysis* 66, no. 1 (2006): 69–76.

Santos, Maciel, and Ana Guedes. "The Profitability of Slave Labor and the 'Time' Effect." *African Economic History* 36 (2008): 1–26.

18. Films and Video Recordings

Include the director's name, the city of production, the production company, and date. Add the medium of publication if the film is recorded on DVD or videocassette.

5. Memento, directed by Christopher Nolan (Universal City, CA: Summit Entertainment, 2000), DVD.
6. Beasts of the Southern Wild, directed by Behn Zeitlin (Los Angeles: Fox Searchlight Pictures, 2012).

Beasts of the Southern Wild. Directed by Behn Zeitlin. Los Angeles: Fox Searchlight Pictures, 2012.

Memento. Directed by Christopher Nolan. Universal City, CA: Summit Entertainment, 2000. DVD.

19. Television Broadcasts
Start with the title of the show; then give the episode number, broadcast date, and network. Include the names of the director and writer.

1. *Mad Men*, episodes no. 53–54, first broadcast March 25, 2012, by AMC, directed by Jennifer Getzinger and written by Matthew Weiner.

Mad Men. Episodes no. 53–54, first broadcast March 25, 2012, by AMC. Directed by Jennifer Getzinger and written by Matthew Weiner.

20. Sound Recordings
Include the original date of recording if it is different from the recording release date, as well as the recording number and medium.

1. Glenn Gould, performance of *Goldberg Variations*, by Johann Sebastian Bach, recorded 1981, CBS MK 37779, 1982, compact disc.

Gould, Glenn. Performance of *Goldberg Variations*. By Johann Sebastian Bach. Recorded 1981. CBS MK 37779, 1982, compact disc.

21. Interviews And Personal Communications
Notes and bibliography entries begin with the name of the person interviewed. Only interviews that are broadcast, published, or available online appear in the bibliography.

7. Louise Erdrich, interview by Bill Moyers, *Bill Moyers Journal*, PBS, April 9, 2010.

8. Ursula K. Le Guin, "Beyond Elvish," interview by Patrick Cox, *The World*, podcast audio, December 13, 2012, http://www.theworld. org/2012/12/beyond-elvish/.

9. Willie Nelson, "The Siver-Headed Stranger," interview by Andrew Goldman, *New York Times Magazine*, December 16, 2012, 12.

10. Herbert Rosengarten, telephone interview by author, January 17, 2013.

Erdrich, Louise. Interview by Bill Moyers. *Bill Moyers Journal*. PBS, April 9, 2010.

Le Guin, Ursula K. "Beyond Elvish." Interview by Patrick Cox. *The World*. Podcast audio. December 13, 2012. http://www.theworld. org/2012/12/beyond-elvish/.

Nelson, Willie. "The Silver-Headed Stranger." Interview by Andrew Goldman. *New York Times Magazine*, December 16, 2012.

22. Book Reviews

The name of the reviewer (if it has been provided) should come first, as shown below:

1. Brian Leiter and Michael Weisberg, "Do You Only Have a Brain? On Thomas Nagel," review of *Why the Materialist Neo-Darwinian Conception of Nature Is Almost Certainly False*, by Thomas Nagel, *The Nation*, October 22, 2012, http://www.thenation.com/ article/170334/do-you-only-have-brain-thomas-nagel.

Leiter, Brian, and Michael Weisberg. "Do You Only Have a Brain? On Thomas Nagel." Review of *Why the Materialist Neo-Darwinian Conception of Nature Is Almost Certainly False*, by Thomas Nagel. *The Nation*, October 22, 2012. http://www.thenation.com/ article/170334/do-you-only-have-brain-thomas-nagel.

23. Blog Posts

Begin with the author's name, if there is one.

1. Karen Ho, "What Will Gioni's Biennale Look Like?," *The Art History Newsletter*, July 20, 2012, http://arthistorynewsletter.com/.

Ho, Karen. "What Will Gioni's Biennale Look Like?" *The Art History Newsletter*. July 20, 2012. http://arthistorynewsletter.com/.

24. Websites

Unless the website is a book or periodical, do not put the site's title in italics. If possible, indicate when the site was last updated; otherwise, include your date of access.

1.   The Camelot Project. University of Rochester, last modified December 21, 2012, http://www.lib.rochester.edu/camelot/cphome.stm.

The Camelot Project. University of Rochester. Last modified December 21, 2012. http://www.lib.rochester.edu/camelot/cphome.stm.

25. Online Videos

Include the author and date of posting, if available, as well as the medium of the source.

1.   Great Ape Trust, "Kanzi and Novel Sentences," YouTube video, January 9, 2009, http://www.youtube.com/watch?v=2Dhc2zePJFE.

Great Ape Trust. "Kanzi and Novel Sentences." YouTube video. January 9, 2009. http://www.youtube.com/watch?v=2Dhc2zePJFE.

26. Tweets

As of this book's press time, Chicago Style recommends that a tweet be described fully in the essay's text, as in the first example below. Following that is, as an alternative, Chicago Style's suggested format for a Twitter feed note citation. There is as yet no guidance for formatting a bibliography entry for a tweet, but one would not go far wrong in following Chicago Style's general guidelines for Web source entries; a suggested example is given in what follows.

Jack Welch (@jack_welch) quickly lost credibility when, on October 5, 2012 at 5:35 a.m., he tweeted that the U.S. Bureau of Labor had manipulated monthly unemployment rate statistics in order to boost the post-debate Obama campaign: "Unbelievable jobs numbers..these Chicago guys will do anything..can't debate so change numbers."[1]

1. Jack Welch, Twitter post, October 5, 2012, 5:35 a.m., http://twitter.com/jack_welch.

Welch, Jack. Twitter post. October 5, 2012, 5:35 a.m. http://twitter.com/jack_welch.

NOTES

1   Harry Frankfurt, *On Bullshit* (Princeton, NJ: Princeton University Press, 2001).

2   Canadians do this on *Cross Country Checkup*, CBC Radio 1, Sundays 3–5 p.m. Eastern Time.

3   See, for example Jeet Heer's application of Frankfurt's ideas in "Donald Trump Is Not a Liar," *New Republic*, 1 December 2015.

4   From the foreword of *Write If You Get Work: The Best of Bob & Ray*, by Bob Elliott and Ray Goulding (New York: Random House, 1975), v.

5   Anonymous translation for The Athenian Society, published in 1898.

6   From *The Problems of Philosophy* (Cambridge: Williams and Norgate, 1912) ch. 15: "The Value of Philosophy." However, he doesn't think it has much success. He argues that philosophy's value is intrinsic.

7   "German Students," 3 November 1933. From R. Wolin, ed., *The Heidegger Controversy* (Cambridge, MA: MIT Press, 1993), ch. 2.

8   *A Discourse on Method* (1637), 2.16.

9   This saying might have originated with E.M. Forster, but there are a dozen other attributions on the Internet.

10   In *On Writing, Editing, and Publishing: Essays, Explicative and Hortatory*, 2nd ed. (Chicago: University of Chicago Press, 1986), 8.

11   Another multiply attributed *bon mot* (see note 9).

12   It was published in "Structure, Sign, and Play in the Discourse of the Human Sciences," in *The Structuralist Controversy*, ed. R. Macksey and E. Donato (Baltimore, MD: Johns Hopkins University Press, 1972), 247–72, at 267.

13   This remark is sometimes misattributed to Foucault, sometimes to John Searle. For what may be the real source, see Stanley Fish's account in *There's No Such Thing as Free Speech and It's a Good Thing Too* (New York: Oxford University Press, 1994), 98.

14   Martin Heidegger, from *What Is Metaphysics?* Quoted by Rudolf Carnap, "The Elimination of Metaphysics through Logical Analysis

of Language," trans. Arthur Pap, in A.J. Ayer, ed., *Logical Positivism* (New York: Free Press, 1932), 69. Originally published in German in *Erkenntnis*, vol. 2.

15 *Contributions to Philosophy (From Enowning)*, trans. Parvis Emad and Kenneth Maly (Bloomington, IN: Indiana University Press, 1989), 307.

16 From "Further Reflections on the Conversations of Our Time," *Diacritics* 27, no. 1 (1997): 13–15.

17 Robert M. Martin, *The Philosopher's Dictionary*, 3rd ed. (Peterborough, ON: Broadview Press, 2002).

18 Steven Weinberg, "Science and Sokal's Hoax: An Exchange," in his *Facing Up: Science and Its Cultural Adversaries* (Cambridge, MA: Harvard University Press, 2001), 161.

19 "This Story Just Won't Write," *The New Yorker*, 19 March 2013.

20 The items on this list, and the one below it, have been gleaned (and sometimes modified) from three excellent works on how to avoid bad writing: *Junk English*, by Ken Smith (New York: Blast Books, 2001), "297 Flabby Words and Phrases That Rob Your Writing of All Its Power," by Shane Arthur (on the web), and *The Broadview Book of Common Errors in English*, by Don LePan (Peterborough, ON: Broadview Press, 2003).

21 "Overstuffed Sentences," by Philip B. Corbett, in a weblog called *After Deadline*.

22 From the precis for "Statistical Predictor Identification," by Hirotugu Akaike, *Annals of the Institute of Statistical Mathematics* 22, no. 2 (1970): 203–17.

23 From the "Argument Clinic," *Monty Python's Flying Circus*, series 3, episode 29, 2 November 1972, BBC Television, written by John Cleese and Graham Chapman.

24 See Richard Doll and A. Bradford Hill, "The Mortality of Doctors in Relation to Their Smoking Habits," *British Medical Journal* 328, no. 7455 (26 June 2004): 1529–33.

25 For some first steps in answering this question, see *Scientific Thinking*, by Robert M. Martin (Peterborough, ON: Broadview Press, 1997).

26 *Monadology, in Discourse on Metaphysics and Other Writings*, ed. Peter Loptson (Peterborough, ON: Broadview Press, 2012), §§32, 36.

27 Aristotle, *Nicomachean Ethics*, trans. Martin Ostwald (Indianapolis: Bobbs-Merrill, 1962), 16.

28 Aristotle, *Politics*, trans. C.D.C. Reeve (Indianapolis: Hackett, 1998), 1.

29 A recent instance: "Beginning to See the Light," by Gary Greenberg, *Harper's Magazine*, March 2016.

30 Quotes from H.L. Menken, in *Minority Report: H.L. Menken's Notebooks* (New York: Knopf, 1956), ch. 373.

31 *Dave Barry's Bad Habits* (New York: Henry Holt, 1985), 202.

32 *Never Eat Anything Bigger Than Your Head and Other Drawings* (New York: Workshop Publishing Co., 1976). This cartoon is easily found in multiple web locations.

33 See his "A Defence of Common Sense" (1925), reprinted in his *Philosophical Papers* (London: Allen & Unwin, 1959).

34 *An Introduction to Philosophical Methods* (Peterborough, ON: Broadview Press, 2010).

35 Thanks to Stephen Latta for most of these suggestions.

36 A.J. Wakefield et al., "Ileal-lymphoid-nodular Hyperplasia, Non-specific Colitis, and Pervasive Developmental Disorder in Children," *The Lancet* 351, no. 9103 (28 February 1998): 637–41 (retracted).

37 R.P. Turco, O.B. Toon, T.P. Ackerman, J.B. Pollack, and C. Sagan, "Nuclear Winter: Global Consequences of Multiple Nuclear Explosions," *Science* 222, no. 4630 (23 December 1983): 1283–92 (retracted).

38 R.P. Turco, O.B. Toon, T.P. Ackerman, J.B. Pollack, and C. Sagan, "Climate and Smoke: An Appraisal of Nuclear Winter," *Science* 247 (January 1990): 166–76.

39 From the *Wikipedia* article.

40 This analysis is presented by Meno, one of the characters in Plato's dialogue by that name.

41 From Kant's *Groundwork of the Metaphysics of Morals* (1785).

42 Versions of this are found in utilitarianism.

43 Examples to this effect are in C. Radford "Knowledge—By Examples," *Analysis* 27, no. 1 (1966): 1–11.

44 How the law might deal with this real-life question is the subject of "Mobile Homes Zoning and Taxation," by Richard W. Bartke and Hilda R. Gage, *Cornell Law Review* 55, no. 4 (April 1970): 491–526.

45 You can Google "1st Ever Humanzee" and find a video, on a website that shows signs of reliability equal to that of the supermarket tabloids.

46 This proof is in his *De rerum natura*, often translated as *On the Nature of Things*, or *On the Nature of the Universe* (1.979–98).

47 Ibid., 1.1060–78.

48 Several versions of this sort of case are discussed in different places. A good discussion of it occurs in Bas C. van Fraassen's *Laws and Symmetry* (Oxford: Oxford University Press, 1998), 217–18.

49 "The Paradoxes of Time Travel," *American Philosophical Quarterly* 13, no. 2 (1976): 145–52.

50   Judith Jarvis Thomson, "A Defense of Abortion," *Philosophy & Public Affairs* 1, no. 1 (Fall 1971): 47–66.

51   See, for example, "Unintended Pregnancy in the United States," by Stanley K. Henshaw, *Family Planning Perspectives* 30, no. 1 (December 1998): 24–29, 46.

52   Source for this story is Richard Brandt, "A Moral Principle about Killing," in *Beneficent Euthanasia*, ed. Marvin Kohl (Buffalo, NY: Prometheus Books, 1972), 108.

53   Adapted from Judith Jarvis Thomson, "The Trolley Problem," *Yale Law Journal* 94 (1985): 1395–1415.

54   Ibid.

55   Lon L. Fuller, "The Case of the Speluncean Explorers," *Harvard Law Review* 62, no. 4 (February 1949): 616–45. This is presented primarily as a legal puzzle.

56   This term was coined by Daniel Dennett in his book *Consciousness Explained* (Boston: Little, Brown, 1991).

57   See, for example, Kathleen V. Wilkes's criticism of thought experiments like Locke's, in *Real People: Personal Identity without Thought Experiments* (New York: Oxford University Press, 1988).

58   David Chalmers, *The Conscious Mind: In Search of a Fundamental Theory* (New York: Oxford University Press, 1996).

59   Hilary Putnam, "The Meaning of 'Meaning,'" in *Philosophical Papers*, vol. 2: *Mind, Language and Reality* (New York: Cambridge University Press, 1985).

60   "Of Identity and Diversity," Bk. 2, ch. 27 of *An Essay Concerning Human Understanding* (1690).

61   "Opening Remarks," in *Of Minds and Language: A Dialogue with Noam Chomsky in the Basque Country*, ed. Massimo Piattelli-Palmarini, Juan Uriagereka, and Pello Salaburu (Oxford: Oxford University Press, 2009), 36.

62   "Hoyle on Evolution," *Nature* 294, no. 5837 (November 12, 1981): 105.

63   Quoted by Paul Davies in his foreword to Simon Mitton's book, *Fred Hoyle: A Life in Science* (Cambridge: Cambridge University Press, 2011), x.

64   *A Theory of Justice* (Cambridge, MA: Harvard University Press, 1971).

65   In *Reason, Truth and History* (New York: Cambridge University Press, 1981), ch. 1.

66   "Philosophy Should Not Be Just an Academic Discipline: A Dialogue with Hilary Putnam," by Hilary Putnam and Janos Boros, *Common Knowledge* 11, no. 1 (Winter 2005): 126–35, at 126.

67   *The Analysis of Mind* (London: G. Allen & Unwin, 1921), 159–60.

68 "Fall in the House of Ussher," in *Eight Little Piggies* (London: Penguin Books, 1993).

69 *Mathematics, Matter and Method* (New York: Cambridge University Press, 1975), 73.

70 *A Treatise of Human Nature* (1739–40), 1.3.6.

71 "What Makes Induction Rational?" *Dialogue* 30: 503–11.

72 *The Problems of Philosophy*, ch. 15 (see above, note 6).

73 This appendix is taken from *The Broadview Pocket Guide to Citation and Documentation*, by Maureen Okun (Peterborough, ON: Broadview Press, 2013), reprinted with the permission of the publisher and author.

GLOSSARY

Here are definitions of the argument-related philosophy-jargon-terms discussed in this book.

a posteriori (Latin: "from what comes after") Knowledge that depends upon sense experience. Contrast with **a priori**.

a priori (Latin: "from what comes before") Knowledge that can be gotten independently of sense experience. Contrast with **a posteriori**.

abduction Another name for—see—**best explanation, argument to the**.

ad hoc assumptions ('Ad hoc' is originally Latin: "for this") Ad hoc means for a specific purpose, without wider application. Saving a theory or a generalization from counter-examples by adding ad hoc assumptions is bad reasoning. The assumptions have to have independent corroboration.

ad hominem (Latin: "to the person") A form of bad argument in which, instead of giving reasons why some proposition is false, one criticizes or attacks the person who proposed it.

ad hominem abusive A form of bad argument in which, instead of giving reasons why some proposition is false, one says abusively negative things about the person who proposed it. (See **ad hominem**.)

ad hominem circumstantial A form of bad argument in which, instead of giving reasons why some proposition is false, one claims that it was proposed because of the special interests of the proposer that it served. (See **ad hominem**.)

ad hominem tu quoque (*Tu quoque* is Latin: "you also") A form of bad argument in which, instead of responding directly to some criticism, one replies by claiming that the criticism applies to the person who made it. (See **ad hominem**.)

agnostic Characterizes a person that neither accepts or denies some position, but claims not to know either way; perhaps the person makes the additional claim that the truth or falsity of that position is unknowable. This word can also describe a belief or system of beliefs which include no judgement about a position. It is most often used regarding the proposition that God exists, so saying that someone is agnostic, without further specifying what she is agnostic about, probably means that she is neither a religious believer nor an atheist.

analysis A philosophical method, or instance of use of that method, in which a word (or its associated concept) is explained by revealing its definition or conceptual structure or application conditions. This technique aims at solving philosophical problems by analysis of key terms associated with that problem.

analytic A statement is analytic when its truth (or falsity) follows merely from the meaning of the words (or the nature of the concepts) involved. Contrast with **synthetic**.

analytic philosophers Originally this referred to those philosophers (mostly Anglo-American twentieth-century) who thought that a productive (or the only productive) method for doing philosophy was **analysis**. When that school of thought lost prominence, this term generalized to cover any philosopher in the dominant twentieth-century Anglo-American tradition, which emphasized argumentative clarity and precision, often relying on formal logic, mathematics, and science. But the increasing diversity in methodology among the philosophers this term is supposed to cover has resulted in a decline in its use. Contrasting methodologies are continental (including existentialism and phenomenology), Thomist, Marxist, and various Eastern systems.

axiom A statement regarded as obviously true or self-evident, or at any rate not in need of defence; presented as the basis for derivation of other statements.

begging the question A bad form of reasoning in which a premise is the same as the conclusion, or presupposes it. This will not serve to convince anyone of the conclusion, because they would not accept all the premises. It's hard to find clear examples of this that don't look just stupid. How about this one: "The rights of the minority are every bit as sacred as the rights of the majority, for the majority's rights have no greater value than those of the minority."

best explanation, argument to the An argument for a conclusion is presented as the best available explanation for what are assumed to be already accepted truths. This is not a form of deductive argument, and is generally not classed as inductive either, though it shares with induction the characteristic that a good argument of that type with true premises does not necessitate the conclusion, but merely makes it more probable.

burden of proof In a philosophical controversy, the person who asserts the truth of some surprising or unorthodox or non-commonsensical or unobvious or debatable proposition is obliged to give evidence to support it. That person is said to have the burden of proof.

common sense The ability to perceive or otherwise arrive at beliefs that are obviously true: "common-sense beliefs."

composition, fallacy of A bad form of reasoning in which the fact that a characteristic pertains to a whole thing is mistakenly taken to follow from the fact that the characteristic pertains to a part of that whole, or to individual things that make up that whole. This is the converse of the **fallacy of division**.

conclusion The statement the truth (or probable truth) of which an argument is meant to establish.

conclusive A conclusive argument (or evidence) is decisive or convincing—not necessarily infallible, but anyway good enough to give rational credibility to the conclusion. Sometimes, however, what's called "conclusive" is an argument or evidence about which there's no possibility of sensible debate or doubt.

confirmed A statement is confirmed by evidence in its favour, and to the extent that there is evidence of this sort. This can fall short of showing that statement definitely, conclusively true. Note that a false statement may nevertheless be confirmed to some degree. Contrast with **disconfirmed**.

counter-argument An argument against a claim made earlier.

counter-example An example intended to show the falsity of an earlier general claim.

deductive argument An argument such that if the premises are all true, then the conclusion has to be true; or, putting the same thing another way: such that the truth of the premises is inconsistent with the falsity of the conclusion. The contrast is with **inductive argument**.

disconfirmed A statement is disconfirmed by evidence against its truth, and to the extent that there is evidence of this sort. This can fall short of showing that statement definitely, conclusively false. Note that a true statement may nevertheless be disconfirmed to some degree. Contrast with **confirmed**.

division, fallacy of A bad form of reasoning in which the fact that a characteristic pertains to a part, or every individual part, of a whole thing is mistakenly taken to follow from the fact that the characteristic pertains to that whole. This is the converse of the **fallacy of composition**.

empirical Having to do with sense-observation. An empirical statement is one whose truth can be, or can in principle be, or has to be, established by sense-observation.

empirically equivalent Two theories or hypotheses are empirically equivalent when there are no observations which, even in principle, could make one more believable than the other.

false cause Any bad sort of reasoning about the cause of something. For a common example, see *post hoc ergo propter hoc*.

hypothesis A supposition or proposed explanation made without much backing, and intended as a starting point for further investigation. An **inference to the best explanation** supports one of several hypotheses by showing empirical evidence in its favour, or that it's the preferable one on other grounds (see **Ockham's razor**).

imply When an argument is deductively valid, then its premises are said to imply its conclusion. Take care to distinguish this from **infer**. We can also be said to imply something when we don't say it, but it follows from, or is suggested by, what we say.

induction by enumeration A form of **inductive argument** for a conclusion of the form *All As are Bs*; the premises point to several particular *As* that are observed to be *Bs*. Another more general form argues from the fact that X per cent of As in the sample are B to the conclusion that X per cent of all As are Bs. Both sorts of argument are stronger when there is a larger number of As in the sample, and when the sample of As is taken at random, or contains a larger variety of other possibly relevant characteristics.

inductive argument An argument in which the premises are jointly consistent with the falsity of the conclusion, but they make the conclusion more credible to some degree. The contrast is with **deductive argument**.

infer What we do when we deduce a conclusion from premises—when we see that the premises imply the conclusion. Take care to distinguish this from **imply**.

infinite regress An infinite regress of support in an argument occurs when a premise A requires support, and would get it from an additional premise B; but then B also requires support, needing C—and so on, apparently with no point appropriate to terminate this series, which heads off uselessly toward infinity. An infinite regress in more general terms is a series in which each object requires one "before" it, and so on.

instrumental value Something has instrumental value when its worth (or part of it) comes from the fact that it is good for something else. Contrast with **intrinsic value**.

intrinsic value Something has intrinsic value when its worth (or part of it) comes from its own nature, rather than from something else that it is good for. Contrast with **instrumental value**.

intuition The process by which we can apparently just realize the truth of some proposition without argument or evidence; an intuition is a proposition known through this process.

intuition pump A thought experiment or other story designed to elicit your intuitions, to clarify them, or make them explicit. But this term is most often used derogatorily: when the story actually narrows your focus and causes you to ignore relevant features, thereby creating intuitions where there were really none to start with. In that case, these pumped intuitions would not be useful for finding philosophical or conceptual truth.

jargon This word can mean technical language, specialized vocabulary (in our case, of philosophy) that usefully abbreviates complicated concepts. It can also mean confused, obscure, pretentious unintelligible language, common enough, unfortunately, in philosophy, but very much to be avoided.

justified belief A belief that one is entitled to hold; its justification makes it credible, more likely to be true. This is not the same thing as true belief. We might have no justification for a belief which is nonetheless true; and we might have considerable justification for a belief which is nonetheless false.

logical form The abstract structure of a sentence relevant to its logical relations with others. This is independent of the content within this structure. Thus, for example, any statement of the form "*A* or *B*" together with the negation of the *A*-statement will validly imply *B*, no matter what the contents of those statements *A* and *B* are.

Ockham's razor A rule for explanation and theory production which states (briefly) that entities should not be multiplied unnecessarily. What this usually means in practice is that an explanation which is less complicated, and/or relies on otherwise acceptable principles and existents, is preferable to one that is more complicated or postulates new principles or entities—all else (notably empirical adequacy) being equal.

only if This is a logical connective that connects two sentences, for example, "Frank is at the party only if he was invited." That means that if Frank is at the party, then he was invited. It does not mean that if he isn't at the party, then he wasn't invited.

ontological parsimony An explanation or theory has this characteristic to the degree that it minimizes the number of different kinds of things whose existence it postulates. Relative ontological parsimony is, according to **Ockham's razor**, one factor in making one theory or explanation preferable to another.

open question A question whose answer has not been provided, or is a matter about which there is significant controversy.

paradox A seemingly false or absurd conclusion that nevertheless appears to follow logically from true premises. Something has gone wrong here.

paradox of justification If every proposition needs a justification, and it's justified by showing that it's logically supported by other propositions, then these other propositions need a justification also, and so on, in an **infinite regress**. The conclusion appears to be that nothing can be justified. The solution: because some assertions obviously are justified, there must be some that don't need justification, or that are justified other than by other assertions.

parallel reasoning It can be shown that one argument is bad by showing that its reasoning is just like—is parallel to—the clearly bad reasoning of another argument. In this book, this is called the "that's just like arguing" argument.

post hoc ergo propter hoc (Latin: "after this, therefore because of this") A form of bad reasoning in which the fact that *B* comes after *A* is taken to show that *A* causes *B*. (More information than this is needed for that conclusion.)

premise Premises are the statements in an argument intended to support the **conclusion**. An older, infrequently encountered, but still acceptable alternative spelling is 'premiss'.

self-evident A self-evident statement is one that is obvious, in need of no justification or evidence in its favour; it's supposed to be evident just on its own.

scepticism In general, a doubting attitude toward a particular proposition or system of beliefs. Sometimes in addition the view that nobody could know the truth/falsity of that proposition or system.

slippery slope A common form of moral argument in which it is claimed that some practice or policy now apparently fairly harmless will inevitably lead to progressively worse practices or policies. Controversy about instances of such arguments usually concentrates on the assumption that worse things are likely to follow.

straw man This sort of argument attacks a proposition or argument by presenting a misstated or misinterpreted or exaggerated version of it—a version easy to knock down.

synthetic A statement is synthetic when its truth (or falsity) does not follow merely from the meaning of the words (or the nature of the concepts) involved. Contrast with **analytic**.

that's like arguing When people criticize someone's reasoning they sometimes say this, and then produce an example of the same sort of reasoning that's obviously no good. The more official name of this sort of critique is "parallel reasoning."

thought experiment This typically involves imagining a story that does not (maybe cannot) really take place. But it's more than just engaging in fictional storytelling; it's supposed to reveal something about the way we think about things. A frequent example involves clarifying or analysing a concept by imagining odd cases to see whether we'd count them as fitting the concept in question or not. In ethics, thought experiments are used to test proposed ethical generalizations.

FROM THE PUBLISHER

A name never says it all, but the word "Broadview" expresses a good deal of the philosophy behind our company. We are open to a broad range of academic approaches and political viewpoints. We pay attention to the broad impact book publishing and book printing has in the wider world; we began using recycled stock more than a decade ago, and for some years now we have used 100% recycled paper for most titles. Our publishing program is internationally oriented and broad-ranging. Our individual titles often appeal to a broad readership too; many are of interest as much to general readers as to academics and students.

Founded in 1985, Broadview remains a fully independent company owned by its shareholders—not an imprint or subsidiary of a larger multinational.

For the most accurate information on our books (including information on pricing, editions, and formats) please visit our website at www. broadviewpress.com. Our print books and ebooks are also available for sale on our site.

On the Broadview website we also offer several goods that are not books—among them the Broadview coffee mug, the Broadview beer stein (inscribed with a line from Geoffrey Chaucer's *Canterbury Tales*), the Broadview fridge magnets (your choice of philosophical or literary), and a range of T-shirts (made from combinations of hemp, bamboo, and/or high-quality pima cotton, with no child labor, sweatshop labor, or environmental degradation involved in their manufacture).

All these goods are available through the "merchandise" section of the Broadview website. When you buy Broadview goods you can support other goods too.

broadview press
www.broadviewpress.com